IT'S ABOUT TIME

It's About Time

It goes by quicker than you think

Laura Feise-Dork

iUniverse, Inc.

New York Bloomington Shanghai

It's About Time
It goes by quicker than you think

iUniverse books may be ordered through booksellers or by contacting:

iUniverse
1663 Liberty Drive
Bloomington, IN 47403
www.iuniverse.com
1-800-Authors (1-800-288-4677)

Because of the dynamic nature of the Internet, any Web addresses or links contained in this book may have changed since publication and may no longer be valid.

The views expressed in this work are solely those of the author and do not necessarily reflect the views of the publisher, and the publisher hereby disclaims any responsibility for them.

ISBN: 978-0-595-50003-1 (pbk)
ISBN: 978-0-595-61337-3 (ebk)

Printed in the United States of America

Laura Elizabeth VanBibber-Roza-Feise 1990

This book is about time but it's not in the order of time.

I began writing when I was seventy-five. Funny, that was about the same time I was becoming a Dork. I never would have thought I would end up a Dork. I am responsible for making all my children Dorks. Let me fill you in on how I became a Dork.

Our friends Pat and her husband Bill talked my daughter Shirley and I into going on a Poker Run with a local club called the Forty Niner Football Club. We went from place to place, on a bus, and picked up playing cards. At each place we got a sealed envelope. I thought I was just playing a fun game, highest hand wins. Little did I know that with out even me realizing it, I was slowly and secretly becoming a Dork.

There were about 30 of us on this little Poker Run, bus trip. We were all having a great time. There was this one man named Glen who always seemed to be showing up right at my side. Before I knew it he was telling everyone that I was "his". I told him, "No way buddy." As it turned out he knew the score better than me.

Well, this guy Glen won the Poker Run with six sixes. Boy was he happy. He asked me if I would like to go to dinner and dancing that night at the Moose Lodge. I consented. After all, he was sort of cute in a mischievous kind of way. My terms though. I would take my own car and meet him there.

We had a very nice dinner. While we were finishing our dinner he dropped the bombshell. He told me he was a Dork. I mean, he told me his last name was Dork. Wow! You could have knocked me over with a feather. It was quite a shock. So many things ran through my head. I was afraid to react. Afraid I would start cracking up right out loud. Whenever my kids did or said something stupid I would say, "Oh don't be such a Dork!"

That ranked right up there with numbskull and knucklehead. I just smiled politely and acted as if it didn't faze me a bit.

After dinner we had a drink and listened to the band. Glen danced the first dance with me. Then he went off to dance with some of the other ladies he knew from the lodge. "Fine with me," I thought to myself. "You want to play that game fella." So I danced with some of the men I knew from the lodge. It just so happens we were both members of the Moose Lodge but had never ran into each other before. By the third dance I got a little tired of the show-off game and retreated to the bar to visit with some of my friends while he was prancing around on the dance floor. We were laughing and joking and having a fun time. They asked me, "Hey, where's your boyfriend?" I said, "No way, he's not my boyfriend." I was just getting ready to go when I heard a voice behind me say, "Hey, where did you run off to?" I told him I was going home. When he asked me what the matter was I told him flat out, "Where I come from, when a man asks a lady out to dinner and dancing he spends most of the time with her". He gave me a cocky smile and said, "Are you jealous?" "Ah, go to your room," I told him. Are you kidding?

There is nothing to be jealous about. I don't even know you and to tell you the truth I don't really think I want to." I picked up my purse and started for the door, I could see out of the corner of my eye he was upset. He touched my arm. "I'm sorry, he said sincerely, I won't do that again." He admitted that he was showing off that he knew so many women. I told him I didn't care how many women he knew, after all, I knew a lot of men from the lodge too. He asked me for my phone number. I wrote my number on a cocktail napkin. Beside the number it said, "Laura, ok me." Years later I saw that little napkin folded neatly in the pages of his address book. Besides my writing he wrote, "Dance Lady". I had to laugh. Right! Dance Lady. One dance and I'm a Dance Lady! I never even told him my last name. I think he thought my last name was OKME. I truly was upset with him that night but I did not want him to know. I tried to act as if it didn't bother me at all. He eventually found out exactly how I felt.

Two days later Glen called my house and low and behold a man answered. He called twice that day and hung up. This went on for three days. He was persistent. Finally, apparently on the last call he had intended to make, I answered the phone. He sounded very happy that I answered but then his tone quickly changed. "Who was that man answering your phone?" he said with a huff. "Why … you jealous?" I said. "Is this some kind of game?" he said. "No, it just turned out that way. How does it feel? I said. Then I told him that the man who had been answering my phone for the past three days was my son Ted. He came down for a visit and got very sick the day after he got here. He ended up staying a month. I invited Glen to dinner the next night. Ted told Glen, "Man, I've been here a week and she never made a special dinner like that for me." Glen was glad he came. Ted left for Mexico shortly after that. When Ted came back I told him Glen had proposed marriage but I wasn't sure. I needed some time to think about it. So what was my answer?

You really didn't think I was going to tell you the end of the story before I even got started did you? I have too much to say, too many things have happened to me in my life. Some stories my children have heard over and over about where I grew up and how I lived. My brothers and sisters lived so far away and they wanted to know all about them. Some stories I'm sure at least some of the kids have never heard. This book is not just a therapeutic exercise for me. It is for my children, and my brothers and sisters. Well, I guess it's for the whole family. Here are the stories I told them, and maybe some I didn't. If I leave anyone out I will apologize right now. That's what happens when you start recalling your life at eighty. Well, here goes kids, this is for you.

So while I'm thinking about it let me take you way back, to the beginning of me.

Preface

Looking back gives me plenty of insight. I realize all the trials and tribulations I went through only helped to mold me into the strong woman I am today. Fortunately, I was wise enough to rely on a very powerful partner that assisted me though every ordeal and that was the LORD. Without the LORD in my life I would not have been able to endure some of the problems I was faced with from time to time. There are so many things that go wrong, even when you think you are doing right but God will always come to your rescue. He actually urges us to draw close to him and promises if we do, he will draw close to us. What a wonderful feeling to have a close relationship with your creator. The longer I live, the more I realize God's plan. Just watching birds and animals shows me that everything was given a brain, down to the smallest living thing, but only we were given the ability to reason. No matter how smart we become, or how much we learn, God knows your plan before you do, but since he gave us free will; he always hopes we will decide for the best which direction to take. My life shows me how strange life really is, the things that happen to me, some I never planned or even dreamed of, made me who I am today; an old lady who loves the life she has. The memories I have stored away are like treasures worth more than gold. Yes, we all live with memories, some are pleasant and some aren't but they all have worth, whether they make you smile or cry. We should remember though, our life is an open book to God, nothing is hidden, and he is always there to help.

One thing I would like to tell young people is to treat life like an adventure. Don't always look for the easy way out, because eventually there isn't one. Listen to someone who has, as you say, "been there, done that." Listening to the voice of experience can save you so much heartache and pain. Believe me; just like the Bible shows us, history repeats itself over and over again. It's always the same thing, just a different day. These days there's just more things to buy and it's usually easy come, easy go.

We all want something and we generally want it now. Whether its wealth or fame or beauty or popularity, unfortunately often it turns out to be a thorn in our side. I wanted so much to be beautiful, like my sister Betty. I thought she had it all. I was reminded constantly by many people how beautiful Betty was and how homely I was. Betty was always treated very special for the way she looked too. Things are still the same. Nothing has changed; the beautiful people are selected, go first, get the recognition, and so forth. The homely are, well they're homely, get to the back of the line you ugly little thing. I remember my Dad saying, "Beauty is only skin deep." I remember thinking, "Boy, my skin must be as thick as a brick." But guess what, I actually turned out to be a very beautiful woman and I didn't even know it until people started telling me I was. More important I now more enjoy, the inner beauty I acquired from the humility I learned, and I have God to thank for helping me with that. It is really who you are, and how you treat people that forms you and makes you pretty or ugly. My brother Warren and I knew a lady that had a growth coming out the side of her neck. It really looked awful. But that lady was so kind and gentle that her inside beauty took over her outside deformity. Mom told me that pretty is as pretty does and she was right. Remember a cherry is beautiful on the outside but look out for the pit, it could bust your teeth out. I remember some of the people I looked up to and admired growing up. From royalty like Queen Elizabeth to all the beautiful movie stars. I watched them all as went though, their trials and tribulations, raised their children, grew old, got wrinkles and gray hair just like me. No matter who we are, rich, poor, pretty or homely we all have to deal with many of the same things. So make your life happy, it is truly a gift from God. Don't worry about what you don't have. Take delight in what you do have, and give thanks to God for it. Some people get very sad about getting old, I refuse to, even though the mirror reminds me every day. I have spoke to her the other day, that lady in the mirror, and asked, "Just who are you?' She replied, "I'm just some old lady you are in charge of taking care of, so do it right, okay?" Believe me, I am trying. The other day she couldn't open ajar. I had to help her before she broke my wrist. Growing old is inevitable, for now anyway. It's strange to watch yourself grow old, but to watch your children grow old is actually a privilege. Some of my very dear friends are dying, that is hard for me. But worse was watching one of my children die. Many dreadful things have happened to me in my life but that is and always will be the worst thing that could ever happen to anyone. It is strange how death can affect you in so many different ways. It's hard to see so many of your loved ones gone and you're not. I have lost my Mom, Dad, three sisters, one brother, oh, and four husbands! Four husbands! I guess I was trying to keep up with one of my favorite movie stars, Elizabeth Taylor.

The Bible tells us that "Time and unforeseen circumstance befalls us all." No one knows when they are going or how but we do know we're going. God does have a plan though and someday death and dying will be no more, he promises that. The world is in such a horrible state it surely can't be too much longer. I remember my Grandmother telling me I wouldn't make it past 13 because she thought the end must be very near. I am now 81. The Bible tells us that no one knows but the Father, not even the angels know when the end will be so I just don't worry about it. He knows the perfect time, he made the plan a long time ago and it will happen when it is supposed to happen. Use your brain to listen to what he tells us now and don't worry about what is going to happen. He has made us aware of all the changes we should expect and be looking for so keep on the watch. I read somewhere that your mind isn't even fully developed until you are about 30, later for some I'm sure. Too bad more teenagers don't enjoy learning. It's a little more difficult when you get older, believe me. I wish I would have had the opportunities that many kids have these days. It saddens me to see many don't take advantage of it. I thought of a good recipe to create one ripe old age:

You start with several cups of LOVE, mix with as much CARE as you can give. Add just enough OIL to keep the joints from going out of whack, sift in quite a few grandchildren to hold things together, keep the heat down so you don't burn but timing is everything because you do want it to be well done. Grannies are good when they are crunchy and sweet so never over-bake.

Now that my children are getting older they are starting to realize that health actually has a little more value than wealth. So I am telling you grandkids, take care of yourself. Stay away from the drugs, cigarettes and take it easy on the alcohol. I know it's been said a million times; fresh air and exercise are important ingredients to a long and happy life. It's true, you have heard this over and over but how do you think you learned your ABC's? Try to make someone happy and you will make yourself happy too. I've said these things to my kids, grandkids, great-grandkids and great, great grandkids. I have so many in my life I had to put them in a spreadsheet to get them all in order. As long as there is a breath in me I will always hold true to the fact that the finest things in life are free. My children have been my finest treasures. I loved watching them development their little personalities one by one, then watching the next one pick up some of the one before or after as well as their own. The best part though was seeing myself in many of them. From time to time I enjoyed seeing how some of them picked up talents or traits that I remembered from my parents. Throughout the years I experienced many changes, hair styles, car styles, books and movies, favorite things, homes, husbands and attitudes. Once my skin was smooth and ivory now it is mapped with experience. My hair has transformed from coal black to grey. But I am the same person inside and I like myself. I started writing this book about my life a few years ago. With the aid of my children and grandchildren I think I have divulged just about everything I can remember or really want to say. Now that I am 81 years old I finally consider myself a beautiful, intelligent, gifted, wealthy person. What more could any woman ask for?

CHAPTER 1

▼

My life began on March 5, 1925 in Omaha Nebraska. My parents, John and Della Van Bibber already had four children. My sister Lela was the oldest. Then came my two sisters Mary and Betty. Betty's real name was Bessie but you wouldn't be too popular if you ever called her that. My brother Albert was next. Everyone called him Al. After me came my brother Warren, then brother Charlie, then came my baby brother Bobby, My Mom finished up with two more girls, Thelma, better known as Teddy and Bonnie Lou. When I was a baby the neighbors said they never heard me cry. Mom said I was her quietest baby. I think it was because I was always in someone's arms. Mary and Lela carried me all the time. They were eight and nine.

"How far back can you remember Mom?" That was a question I got many times from my children. I guess my earliest recollection was about three years old. I remember digging in the dirt under the porch with my brother Warren. Warren and I spent a lot of time together. We didn't have a room full of toys like kids today. We were very poor. The depression started in 1929, I was four years old.

I remember my brother Al made a wagon for Warren, Charlie and I. We all piled in it and Al pulled us across the street so we could watch the trains go by. We were all mesmerized by the size and rumbling of the giant rail cars. Warren and Charlie got out of the wagon for a closer look. I felt safer staying in the wagon. But I wasn't. Shortly after they got out and car came speeding around the corner out of nowhere and hit the wagon with me in it. My brothers watched in horror as the car drug me down the street a ways. The young man driving came to a stop and jumped out of the car. His face was white and his hands were shaking. He pulled me out from under the car. There was blood all over me. I looked much worse than I was. I remember the terror in my mother's eyes as my brothers walked me through the door. I thought her eyes were going to pop out of her head. She put my head under an outside pump and washed the blood away. I had a bad cut on my head. The bone still sticks out of my head. Yes, I suppose I was one of the original boneheads.

On my fifth birthday mom made me a cake. I got the first piece. I'll never forget the thrill I felt when a nickel fell on my plate. I wondered how she knew where the nickel was. What a smart mom.

I was put in the hospital a short time after that. I had malnutrition. I was in the hospital for one month. I do not know how this happened. I was a real shy child. Maybe no one was paying attention to me and I was not eating. The stay in the hospital seemed forever to me, one whole month. I don't remember much about the stay except there were ten little beds, five on each side. I remember a little boy who must have been about seven or eight. He would come and tease all of us when the nurse left. I sure felt lonely. When mom or dad came I cried to go home. I could not understand why I had to stay there. When Mom finally came to pick me up she brought me a pretty dress. I remember we walked one block to the streetcar. Boy was I happy to be going home.

For some reason as soon as I walked in the front door it felt like something was different. I didn't realize mom was going to have another baby. I never even noticed how big she was getting. She always looked the same to me, just my pretty mom.

Then the time arrived. It was a warm day in September. Lela and Mary were in the house with mom and dad. I didn't know then why the rest of us were told to stay outside.

Betty, Warren, Charlie and I were sitting under a big tree and Al was running around when Dad came out and told us we had a baby sister. Thelma Jean was her name and I thought she was the most beautiful baby I had ever seen. I saw a doctor come in with a black bag. I actually thought he brought little Thelma Jean in it. We started calling her Teddy and it stuck with her all through her life. So much commotion was going on around our house but I tuned it all out when I was around my new baby sister. I loved standing by her crib and just watching her.

It was the fall of 1930 and the day came for me to start school. Mom made me a pretty dress with panties to match. She was very resourceful, she made them out of flour sacks. Actually they were very pretty sacks. We got our flour in hundred pound sacks and the sacks had pretty cloth patterns. Mom made everything out of them. Scarlet O'Hare had her drapes, mom had her flour sacks.

Mary took me to school on my first day and I cried all the time. They asked Mary to take me home. Mary tried to talk me into going back but I said no way. When we got home mom said I had to go back to school and not cry or I would get a spanking. The next day Mary took me back. I didn't cry but I was frightened. My teacher had a real neat way of making us want to come back to school and feel good about being there. She had these little red chairs that were just our size. She let us pick out the one we wanted and that was ours for the rest of the school year. Funny, a little thing like that made school fun for me.

The year was 1932. Hoover was President. The Great Depression was in full swing. Times were hard. I really never new any different that was just the way it was.

Another baby came to our house, Bonnie Lou. I wondered where mom and dad found such beautiful babies. We had a little wood stove in our kitchen called a monkey stove. It was about two feet high. Mom and Dad heated bricks on it to put around Bonnie Lou to keep her warm. I guess it was like a homemade incubator. I remember them putting Bonnie Lou in cold water, then in hot water to make her breath. They were praying for her life and crying. Warren, Charlie and I were huddled together watching. It was a very sad sight. Thelma Jean (Teddy) was five when Bonnie Lou was born. I will always remember Bonnie Lou. She only lived one month. I got to hold her. Her little fingers wrapped around my finger. I remember Mom and Dad praying for her life. They took her away and I never saw her again. No one knew how hard it was for me. They never even told me where they took her. I just listened to them talking as I lied in bed one night. I heard them say that she died. Boy did I cry. This is when I realized that our Mom and Dad really loved us. Mom sounded so sad. They never really told us they loved us, I just knew it. There were nine children in our family; Lela, Mary, Al, Betty, Warren, Charlie, Teddy and me. Oh, I always included Bonnie Lou. She might have only lived for one month but she was my little sister regardless.

I remember the time our house was under quarantine, well part of it anyway. Warren and Charlie came down with double pneumonia. Mom and Dad made tents for them in our living room. No one could go in there. Even with all my other siblings I felt very alone without Warren and Charlie. Maybe Mom and Dad didn't tell us they loved us with spoken words that I can remember but I do remember how they took care of us when we were sick. I had a number of earaches as a child. I recall Dad holding me on his lap and putting something hot in my ear. I didn't know what it was then but I found out later they warmed some oil up on a spoon and poured it in my ear. Later on my kindergarten teacher informed my parents that I was deaf in one ear.

Looking back I appreciate the extra time that teacher took to help me with my affliction. She taught me to listen with my right ear and a whole new world opened up for me.

I was quite a tomboy. Even though I enjoyed playing with dolls once in awhile I preferred playing marbles, climbing trees with Warren and Charlie. I say dolls, I should have said doll. I only had one growing up and she was a pretty sad looking doll but I loved her. I didn't give her up until I was ten. I think she fell apart to tell you the truth.

I used to like climbing on the railroad cars that sat on the tracks near our house. I liked drawing too. I used to use the edges of the newspaper to draw on. I never really cultivated my artistic side until I was older. I take that back. I did draw several cartoons for my friend across the street. Actually she was my little sister Teddy's friend, her name was Patsy Flaxbeard. When Patsy realized I could draw pretty good she brought be drawing paper. She brought some for me and some to draw cartoons on for her. I really don't remember much of what I drew but I remember doing some kind of series of cartoons. They must have been pretty good because every week Patsy would come over and get her cartoon.

There was always something going on at our house. It seems like someone was always getting sick or hurt. One day Warren cut his wrist real bad. I don't remember who it was but somebody told him his hand was going to have to be amputated. As it turns out all he needed was some stitching up and he came home smiling. He sure got a lot of attention over that stunt.

One time Al and Warren were cutting weeds in our back yard, both had a scythe. A scythe is a tool that cuts grass or weeds. It has a handle about four feet long with a large blade at the end for cutting or hacking. Al was bent down and Warren hacked Al right in the head. Off to the doctor again but this time it was Al. He was in pain for a long time. Mom put flour on it to stop the bleeding. I know that sounds funny but it worked. Mom used a lot of home remedies.

Warren and I were very close, where you saw one the other was not far behind.

It was 1933. There was a nightclub across the street from our house, Piccolo Pete's. Warren and I would go over and ask the customers if we could watch their car. We charged a nickel. No one ever turned us down. We always got our nickel and no one ever lost a car. We were seven and eight then. Mom and Dad never knew about our secret little enterprise. We were always playing outside at night, and always looking for a way to make some money.

Generally Warren, Charlie and I always walked to school together. There was one time though, Warren and Charlie were both sick and I had to walk alone. I made it to school all right but on the way home I was faced with a situation that, depending on how I reacted, probably meant my life. I remember a big green car and there was a man driving. He pulled up along side of me and rolled down the window. He said hello and asked me if I would like to have the big doll that was in his back seat. I looked in the back seat. It was the biggest, most beautiful doll I had ever seen. But I was getting a nagging feeling that something just wasn't right. I remembered overhearing a conversation Mom and Dad had about a little girl named Mary Jean Parker. A man offered her a doll. I guess she made the mistake of getting in the car with him. The man took Mary Jean home and dismembered her in his bathroom. At that moment, a horrible, graphic vision of Mary Jean Parker saved my life. I ran as fast as I could and never looked back. I never told anyone either. I always somehow thought that, in a way, Mary Jean saved my life.

I was so happy when Warren and Charlie were well enough to go to school again.

The first of my siblings to get married was my oldest sister Lela. In 1934 she married a man named Harold Cunningham. They were quite a pair. Lela was a little tiny woman like Mom. Harold was over six feet tall, a giant of a man to us. He was a big man, but he was a gentle man. Warren and I loved him. He was just like our big brother. I saw more of Lela after she married Harold than I remember seeing her when she lived at home. She always showed her love for us when we stopped by and visited them. She always welcomed us with open arms. We loved her hugs and her peanut butter sandwiches.

My sister Mary got a job at St Joseph Hospital. I remember a lady that worked in the kitchen that would always give us a meal when we went to visit Mary. She told us many times how much she enjoyed working with Mary.

Mary moved in with a family that needed someone to care for their mentally disabled daughter. Her name was Janet. Mary cared for her very much, like a little sister. She even brought Janet over to our house one time.

Mary was always doing something nice for someone. One time she bought me a snowsuit. I remember that suit like I got it yesterday, brown and orange plaid top and brown pants. I will never forget the time Mary bought me a very much-needed pair of shoes so I would have something nice to wear to school. I didn't want to take them off. I secretly wanted a pair of Mary Jane's; black patent leather with a strap over the arch. I know if I had told her she would have bought me a pair. We were taught never to ask for anything though. Mary was a very loving sister. She always hugged me whenever she came home and told me how much she loved me. She never knew how good it made me feel. Who wouldn't love a sister like that? Hey Mary, if I never told you enough, I LOVE YOU. I really never got that kind of affection from my parents. Thank God for my loving sisters and brothers.

Al moved away from home to work with a man who had an auto shop. Al was a very handsome young man. He had dark brown eyes, coal black hair and a beautiful smile. He was a very quiet person. He stayed to himself quite a bit but he always looked out for me. He lived with that man for three years. I didn't see much of him during that time. I sure did miss him.

C H A P T E R 2

▼

During the depression, to help feed the family, some of us kids sold candy. Mary and Al sold it first. I didn't remember that, Mary told me. Then when I was nine and Warren was eight we took over the job of selling candy. Times were rough. Even though things were cheap, bread was a nickel a loaf; money was hard to come by. Selling candy made us feel like we were helping. Besides that, it made for some pretty exciting adventures and wonderful memories for Warren and I.

There were so many _Rocky Roads_, too numerous to count. We could never keep track of all the _Mounds_ we had to hurdle. Sometimes we felt like we were from _Mars_. We were just two _Power House_ kids doing the best we knew how. If we got real hungry a _Denver Sandwich_ really made our day. _Three Musketeers_ is what we were. Even if we were only two we always knew Jesus was on our side, watching us and helping us along the way. We were always together, Warren and me. We were _Forever Yours_. We laugh today thinking of how the candy actually saved our day. We made up songs of candy and sang them on our candy route. This made our day _Whiz_ by. We would always get the biggest laugh when we ran into _Mr. Goodbar_. He was by far the nuttiest. _Oh Henry_ and _Baby Ruth_ gave him a lot of competition though as far as being nutty. We loved them all but _Bit O' Honey_ was the sweetest to us. At the end of the day thought, _Payday_ put them all to shame. Who doesn't like a big fat _Payday_? Without _Payday_ we couldn't turn around and do it all again the next day.

Your can have fun in life no matter how rough things are for you. You just have to find it. Make your life happy as you go along. There will always be something you can't handle, but you can always turn it over to God. Through the good times and the bad, he will always be there for you. We did not realize it at the time but those candy bars made Warren's and my life bearable. Life is a bowl of cherries, just watch out for the pits.

Warren and I were like Orville and Wilbur, Burns and Allen, and Lewis and Clark all wrapped into one. We were quite a candy-selling team. We would do anything or go just about anywhere to make our quota for the day. For one dollar we set off on our journey with twenty-five candy bars. If we sold two bars each we brought home five dollars each. After school we would each receive two boxes of candy and off we would go I cringe today when I think of some of the places we went to sell that candy. One of the places we used to hang around was the railroad tracks. This is where we met the first black man we really ever knew. His name was Pretty Like A Rose. He picked up the coal that had dropped off the railcars and was laying alongside the tracks. I remember him telling us "What you two kids doin' down here. Don't cha know how dangerous it is. Stay off the tracks and look out for the trains. You could get really bad hurt out here." He was always looking out for us. Turns out somebody should have been looking out for him. One day there were a lot of people on the railroad tracks because someone had been hit by a train. We were so sad when we found out it was Pretty Like A Rose. His body was in pieces. They were picking him up when we arrived. Warren actually found his jawbone. They sent us out of there. No one knew he was our friend. We were very upset but we couldn't tell anyone because we weren't even supposed to be anywhere near the tracks, or talk to strangers. Kind of a difficult thing to do since we lived very near the railroad tracks and the only way we were going to sell all our candy was to talk to at least some people we didn't know.

But Pretty Like A Rose was never a stranger to us. He always seemed like a friend; even from the first day we met him. We always looked forward to seeing him. He was always there. When we went by this big fuel company called the Gas Works he would always yell out for us to be careful and watch out for the trains. We would always wave to him and say, "Okay, Pretty Like A Rose". We loved his name. Warren and I found the biggest candy bar we had. We tore off the wrapper and split it. "This is for Pretty Like A Rose," we said as we cried and ate it. We were so very sad that we would never see him again. He helped us to be aware of the tracks. Warren and I always thought that in some way, Pretty Like A Rose saved our lives. That could have been us. We knew we would be in big trouble if we told our parents about him so we never did.

One of the most dangerous places we went to sell candy was the Gas Works. This place was full of burning vats. We walked over planks with fire burning down below. Warren and I stayed very close together. It was dangerous but we had to go there. That's where we sold most of our candy. We had a five-mile radius to sell our candy. We went two miles a day. Sometimes our route would take us right pass our sister Lela's house. This was a great place for a break. Lela would always fix us up with a couple of peanut butter and jelly sandwiches. Boy did they taste good. To this day, every time I have a great PB&J I think of my sister Lela. She was so kind to us. We were so glad she married Harold. He was like a brother to us. The store around the block from Lela and Harold's house sold candy bars, three for a dime. This is where we would replenish our supply. We were pretty good salesmen because most of the time we sold all our candy before we got home.

One of our steady customer's was the "goiter lady". She worked in a big office. She had a huge growth on her neck but she was really nice. She would always buy a candy bar. Then she would tell us to pick out our favorite kind and she would buy one for us. She always made us tear the wrapper and start eating it before we left. She made sure we enjoyed it. I think she knew that we would probably go out and re-sell it. We will never forget her. We never even knew her name. Names were not important to us, we knew everybody by face.

The weather in Omaha, Nebraska was hot in the summer. In the winter there were tornados, rain and snow. It was so cold. I remember one time we were out selling candy and a big wind came up. The sky was almost totally black. We heard a tornado was coming. Low and behold Warren and I looked across the field and there was a big funnel cloud heading our way. In the distance trees were falling like they were toothpicks. Warren and I crawled under some steps until it passed. Warren was ten and I was eleven. For such small children we knew what to do. I guess it was drilled into to our heads from a very early age since we always had tornados. It seems like we even had it over the United States Postal System. They only delivered mail through wind and rain and dead of night, or something like that. Nothing stopped us when it came to selling candy; not even tornados! Nothing seemed to bother Warren. I always thought I was just as strong but the truth is, he made me brave.

Another favorite place for a sure candy sale was the Kiddy Clover Potato Chip Factory. Not only did we sell candy there, we also got some pretty good deals. A big bag of broken potato chips or a bag of day-old rolls from the bakery was ours for just a dime. This was quite a treat for the whole family and Warren and I were so pleased and proud that we could bring something home that everyone enjoyed.

CHAPTER 3

▼

I guess Mom and Dad didn't have enough to take care of because in 1935 another new baby appeared at our house. That was the third new baby and I still thought they came in a little black bag. I don't even remember Mom being pregnant. My dad brought out a basket from the bedroom. Warren, Charlie and I looked in the basket. I remember being puzzled and excited at the same time. I was now ten years old. "Another baby?" I said. I remember everyone laughing. I heard there was a family who had five babies at one time, all girls. I thought they must have had to get a very large black bag for them.

Our new baby was a boy. Mom and Dad named him Robert. Robert Lindy Van Bibber. They gave him the middle name of Lindy after Charles Lindberg. I remember hearing about the Lindberg's baby getting kidnapped. I was so sad to hear that when they found him he was dead. How horrible. I could not understand why someone would want to steal someone's little baby and then let it die too. Charlie also was named after Charles Lindberg. Warren John got his names from Warren G. Harding and Dad. I was named after my two Grandmas'; Laura, my Mom's Mom and Elizabeth was my Dad's mother's name. I like the name Laura Elizabeth but no one ever called me that. My name from a very early age was Lolly. Betty was named after our Aunt Bessie. Boy did she hate that name, so Betty became her name. That named suited her better anyway. I don't blame her. Bessie kind of sounds like a cow and Betty was no cow. With those gorgeous black curls and big blue eyes she was beautiful. I always thought she was special. Apparently so did everyone else. I guess you could say she was pampered. Betty really never was expected to do anything. Then there was me, plain Jane, or so I thought. I had straight black hair, always cut short and was very shy. Betty wasn't really shy but she was, well, different. I remember she had the strangest habit of sleepwalking.

One time I watched her get up out of bed, sit at the mirror and brush her beautiful black hair, put on her robe and walk right out the front door. I told Dad and he just went out and turned her around and headed her right back to her bed without even waking her up.

My sister Lela was named after an aunt on my Mom's side. Mary got her name from Grandpa Albert's cousin. Al got Grandpa Albert's name. Thelma was named after an Aunt in the family. We never did call her Thelma. I always remember calling her Teddy. I guess that's where I got the habit of nicknaming people. I really don't know where Bonnie Lou got her name.

Dad told many stories about our family. On Sunday evenings we looked forward to his stories. One time he told us that Daniel Boone's brother married an aunt of his, Olive Van Bibber. According to Dad they looked after Daniel Boone's family while he was off on his adventures.

I remember my Grandma and Grandpa visiting many times. Grandpa said he would give me a nickel if my face was clean when they came. Believe me, I washed my face in a hurry when I knew they were coming. I guess my face must have been dirty quite a bit. One day the pipes were frozen and we didn't have any water. I looked out the window and saw Grandpa and Grandma coming towards the house. I ran and grabbed some of my mother's cold cream and cleaned my face. I wanted that nickel bad.

Grandpa told us about the time a cowboy hit him on the head with the butt of his gun and left him for dead. A group of Indians picked him up and took care of him for about a year. His family thought he was dead.

Grandpa said his cousin was Mary Todd Lincoln, Abraham Lincoln's wife. He also said he never knew her. My Grandpa was a real sharp dresser. He always wore a suit. How I remember him the best was when he was dressed in his suit with the pink shirt and a big white cowboy hat. He had a great smile. I heard later he was a real "lady's man". He always took time for me. He was a wonderful Grandpa. One time he was hit by a car and had to wear a full body cast. He was in the hospital for a whole year. Mary took care of both Grandma and Grandpa when he got out of the hospital. He cut the body cast off himself. He never fully recovered from that accident. He must have known he was not going to live long because he told me to cake care of Grandma when he was gone. I wondered where he was going.

In 1936 Franklin Roosevelt was running for his second turn and Landan was his running mate. Warren and I heard a song "Roosevelt, Roosevelt, ring the bell,

Landan, Landan, go to hell". We used to sing this song and laugh, by ourselves of course. If mom or dad heard us we would have been in big trouble.

Sunday was for church. Dad gave us each two cents. Warren, Charlie and I went together. We bought as much candy as we could with one penny and put the other in the collection plate. We knew this was wrong but we were always so hungry. I know now that Dad did the best he could to take care of us. I guess that's why we didn't mind selling candy to help out.

Lela had a baby boy. I still didn't know where they came from and I was close to twelve by now. I still thought they came in by way of his little black bag. She named her little boy Howard. Oh how we loved him. Lela let us hold him when we stopped by for our peanut butter and jelly sandwich. I think the reason Warren and I were so close was because we never got to see the rest of the family much. We were always away from home; at school or out selling candy.

We moved to East Omaha in 1937. Lela, Harold and little Howard moved to California. We never had to sell candy anymore after that. I guess the depression was over. I sure missed my sister Lela, Harold and Howard. Times were a little better but there still was not enough work in Omaha for Harold. In 1938 Dad bought a store where we sold furniture. He ran the store while he was still working as foreman at Miller's Cereal Mill. Later on Kellogg's ended up buying the mill. Dad made seventeen dollars a week, not much for a family as large as ours. I said Dad ran the store, but I was the one that worked in it all the time. I had absolutely no time for myself. Between taking care of Grandma and working in the store I was busy all the time. There was a lady that lived across the street from the store, Mrs. Keeley. She was very nice to me. She liked me. I liked her too. She always brought me cookies or candy that she had made. She never had any children of her own. I think she kind of adopted me. I never forgot her and I know she never forgot me. She was always so encouraging to me. I used to confide to her that I would like to have a job somewhere else besides taking care of Grandma and working in the store but I was sure no one would hire me. I had no experience in anything. I was green as moss. She used to tell me I was stronger than I thought. She gave me the courage to look for a job. She told me if I stayed in my Dad's store I would never really grow up and be an independent woman. She was right. I ended up working in that store until I was nineteen and I was still a little girl. I was growing through the books Dad brought into the store. Mom took care of the house and family. Mom made the best apple dumplings I ever ate and no one could make bread better than her. But *anybody* could cook better. Sorry, but Mom was an awful cook. Maybe it was because she could not get everything she needed to make the meal right.

Christmas was coming so Warren and I asked Dad for enough money to buy candy to sell. We told him we would pay him back from what we sold. He gave us enough to buy four boxes. We had to go by streetcar to go to our old places. As usual, we still had what it took. We paid dad back and had enough money to buy everyone something, including Grandma and Grandpa. We even had enough money to buy all the ingredients to make a nice dinner. What a fun time it was for Warren and me. We always got a sock with an orange, an apple, and some nuts. We were happy to get anything.

Warren and I grew up fast. We thought we were full-grown at eleven and twelve. In some ways we were. In others, at least for me, I was still a little child. We thought we could do anything. Boy did I learn later in life just how little I knew.

Grandpa died. I always thought I was a little more special to Grandpa that the rest of my brothers and sisters. I guess it was that dirty face thing we had going.

I loved him so much. Warren and I wanted to see Grandpa but they said we were too young. We thought were full-grown, just like any kid today thinks. So, the dynamic duo, took off by ourselves and went to the mortuary. We saw Grandpa alright. Not a happy site. He looked like he was sleeping but we knew he was dead. I wish I would have just been satisfied to remember the man with the fancy suit, the big white cowboy hat and the wonderful smile.

I graduated from grade school that same year. I was thirteen. I was supposed to give a speech at my graduation but I didn't have anything decent to wear. Mom managed to get one dollar and fifty cents and bought me a dress and a pair of shoes. That was real nice of Mom but I looked like I was ten years old. Looking back I sure was proud of mom coming up with the money to help me. All my friends were decked out in dresses that made them look beautiful and a lot older too. I had a wonderful teacher who helped me be proud of myself no matter what I wore. It was getting close to the time for me to get up and give my speech. I did not want to get up there. I thought I was going to look like a fool. My teacher told me I should be proud of who I was, not what I was wearing. She said, "Clothes do not make the person my dear, it's what's in your heart that matters." I gave the speech and I stared at her the whole time. I really didn't know anyone else in the audience anyway, no one in my family came to my graduation. My classmates were there though.

In 1939 Mary married a man named Noland. Soon after, their first baby boy Petie was born. Lela had a baby girl in California that same year. She named her Evelyn. Time was moving fast. Grandma came to live with us. She was paralyzed on one side and she needed someone to help her do just about everything. So

Grandma became my responsibility. I took care of all her needs, which included bathing her before I went to school and when I got home. Quite a bit to ask of a thirteen-year-old child but there was no one else who could or would do it. It never seems to bother me, at first anyway. I just accepted it as something I had to do. I had so much energy and Grandma got all of it. When I came home from school each day, Grandma was my first chore. Grandma became the top priority in my life. I remember one time Dad and I were talking about aging. He said, "You never know, you might live to be older than Grandma." In my young mind I couldn't even imagine being old like Grandma and she was only fifty-nine at that time. Grandma's pension was a whole twenty-three dollars a month plus what they called commodities. Warren and I would go by streetcar to pick up her commodities once a month. It was very hard for two little kids, even two go getters like Warren and I. It helped us to be stronger though.

As I think back about Mom, I guess you could say she had a pretty easygoing nature. She really only had one friend that I know of, Malder Van Divandi. I'm sure that's not the correct spelling but that's how I remember her name sounded like. She was an outgoing lady. She used to encourage Mom to stick up for herself. She used to tell mom "You have rights you know". Dad didn't like her and he let Mom know it. That didn't stop Mom from spending time with her though. They were together a lot. I used to hide behind the door and listen to them talk. This is how I learned about Mary Jean Parker. Children were not supposed to hear about things like this. It was a good thing I did though as it turns out. I always wished I could have been on the other side of that door and a bigger part of my Mom's life. However you spell it I was glad for the friendship my Mom had with Mrs. Malder Van Divandi. She made my Mom strong, the way she needed to be. I never thought she would stand up to Dad. Sometimes she needed too. We all need to stick up for ourselves once in awhile. Malder helped her to do that.

By 1940 Warren and I were teenagers and Warren got a bit rebellious. Warren was so bull-headed he would even challenge Dad, which was not a very smart thing to do. Dad ruled our house with an iron hand and what he said was law. I always wanted to please Dad, partly because I was a mild mannered child for the most part. But the razor strap he had hanging by the door was a constant reminder of who was boss. I don't ever remember getting hit with that razor strap but Warren sure did. Dad and Warren butt heads all the time. It sure hurt me when Warren got a spanking. I remember Warren telling my Dad, "Go ahead, hit me again, I'm not going to cry." It used to scare me to death because Dad would hit him again and again. I was so afraid he was going to hurt him seriously.

I even would beg Dad to stop. Charlie used to get the strap too but he would take it and not talk back to Dad. I know Dad loved us and did the best he could.

Mary had a little boy and named him Dicky. Our family was growing. I would baby sit for Mary sometimes. She had a very unhappy relationship with Nolan. He was always mistreating her. I was afraid of him. When she went in to have her third child I baby sat Pattie and Dicky. I remember Nolan coming home drunk and was pounding on the door. I just kept the door locked and prayed he wouldn't get it. Mary was such a nice person. I couldn't understand why Noland treated her so bad. I couldn't understand why she stayed with him either. Mary brought home another baby boy, Gary.

CHAPTER 4

▼

In 1941 we got the shock of our lives, World War II. I remember the day. President Roosevelt was on the radio telling us we were at war with Japan. The Japanese bombed Pearl Harbor in a sneak attack. My brother Al was drafted. How I hated to see him go off to war. I would miss him very much. He can been coming around to visit quite a bit just before he was drafted and I was getting very used to his company. I saw him only once after that. He lived in California. He always wrote to me.

Lela had another baby girl and she named her Elnora. They nicknamed her Butchie. She didn't mind the nickname that is, up until she was about twenty-five. Then all of a sudden none of us could call her that or she would get upset. Most of us complied, except for her brother Howard. I think he still calls her that from time to time.

By the time I was a junior in high school I was working in my Dad's second hand store so much that Dad made me quit school and run the store full time. Even though I was sad to be leaving school, I kind of enjoyed working in the store. I was still taking care of Grandma when I wasn't working in the store and oh yes; I did Uncle Oscar's laundry too. Uncle Oscar lived in a room behind the store. We lived upstairs. Uncle Oscar gave me a dollar a week for doing his laundry. With that I bought Warren, Charlie and I a foot long hot dog and a bottle of Pepsi once a week. It was something we all looked forward to.

The store was kind of like my own little private living quarters. I had fun arranging the furniture just how I wanted it. Not too many people could afford to buy new furniture at that time so we were pretty busy. Mrs. Keeley came to visit me quite often. She never bought anything but we sure enjoyed visiting together in my little home away from home. My little sister Teddy visited me in the store sometimes when her friend Patsy Flaxbeard came over. My little brother Bobby was usually with my Mom.

Actually there were several ladies that used to actually buy things and stay to visit. I must admit it was quite cozy in that little store. I always kept everything dust and clutter free. The furniture was always arranged to suit my taste and I would even light candles. Dad never cared how I fixed it up. He gave me total freedom in that regard. Even when there weren't any customers I enjoyed myself by cuddling up to one of the many books that were available in the store. These books not only took me to different places all around the world but they helped me grow so much as a person. I always had something interesting to talk about when the ladies came by for a visit. I can't help but think that my efforts to keep the store well arranged paid off in the long run in sales as well as a fun place to be.

We moved to Council Bluffs, Iowa in 1942. We were just across the river from Omaha. Dad bought another store. It had rooms in the back. My sister Mary had a baby girl. She named her Dolly after our Mom Della. My sister Betty married Bob. Betty had a baby boy. I never saw Al or Mary and her family much. Lela and Betty were far away. Mary had a baby boy named Johnnie.

Uncle Oscar didn't move with us but Grandma did so I still kept busy taking care of Grandma when I wasn't working in the store. Grandma didn't have a clue how busy I was running the store. Sometimes I would be busy for an hour or two before I got back to her. She would be very upset with me. It really didn't bother me so much though because I loved Grandma and I always would do anything she needed me to do, no matter how busy or tired I was.

Betty's husband Bob was in the Army and was sent to California. Betty wanted to go and visit him so she left her little boy Bobby at our house for fourteen months. Little Bobby became a big part of my life, as if there were any parts left. He followed me everywhere. It felt as if Bobby was my little boy. I loved him so much. I potty trained him; I fixed him up a spot to play in the store when I was working. People thought he was mine. He was always at my side.

Sunday was the only day I was free as a bird. It was church then a movie. Dad would give us fifteen cents and off we would go, Warren, Charlie and me. Charlie sometimes would go with Dad to buy furniture.

One Sunday while we were out at the movies, Betty and Bob came to pick up Bobby. This is when my world fell apart. They took my little Bobby without even letting me know. I didn't even get to say goodbye. I just came home and he was gone. For some reason no one even thought of my feelings or little Bobby's for that matter. I was the one who took care of him all those months while they were away. He was my world. I just couldn't believe it. I cried for days on end. Mom and Dad thought I was being silly because he wasn't mine and I just had to let it go. I used to think poor Bobby must have been thinking I just gave him away. They took him and moved to California. I never saw him again until he was three years old. He didn't even know me. I was so lonesome with little Bobby gone. I cried my eyes out with each little toy I picked up of his. I had to move a whole living room set into his play area just to forget about how much I missed him.

Warren was put in charge of the other store Dad bought. We were sixteen and seventeen and both responsible storekeepers. Warren was like me. He kept his store dusted and shined and well arranged. The store hours were 7 am to 9 pm. We did it all; kept the books and dealt with the money. We talked everyday over the phone and compared notes on items and sales. We were very honest too. Except for this one time, which I always felt guilty for. I sold a table for ten dollars more that what Dad priced it for. I kept the ten dollars. I never knew why I did such a thing. How was I going to spend it without getting caught? Where was I going to spend it anyway, and on what? Well, I never was so happy when the lady returned the table and wanted her money back. Boy was I glad I still had that ten dollars. I never did anything like that again. 1944 became a year that Warren and I seemed to both need our freedom at the same time. Warren wanted to join the Marines. Dad said no way, he was too young. Warren was seventeen. Warren rebelled and told Dad he wasn't going to run the store anymore. Dad signed for him to go in the Marines. With Warren and Bobby gone everything changed for me. I told Dad I was going to go to work somewhere else. Dad told me about Social Security. He said they were starting a plan so when you turn sixty-five your can get a pension if you pay into it. I told him, "Then I need to go to work now, so when I get as old as Grandma I will have enough money to take care of myself." The next day I went to the Post Office to get my Social Security card, that's where you got them then. I felt a bit strange being away from the store but at the same time, it was exhilarating.

President Roosevelt was starting another plan at that time. It was called W.P.A., a work program. You were provided a job, along with grants for food and other things. You had to fill out papers every month to stay on the program. I guess it was the beginning of the Welfare System. It did help a lot of people take care of their families. They also had soup kitchens where people could work and help feed their families.

This is why I wanted to go to work. I didn't want to be on welfare. Not that I thought people were bad that were on the program, I just knew I could take care of myself.

I read an ad in the paper that sounded like a good opportunity for me.

The Tip Top Curler Factory was looking for some help.

When I told Dad about it, he wasn't exactly encouraging. In fact he kind of laughed and told me I didn't have any experience and said I would have little chance of getting the job. I think that lack of encouragement gave me that much more determination to get that job no matter what. I know now that running my Dad's store was a very positive part of my past. It helped me grow up. After a while though, just like any normal young adult, I longed for something more. I needed a real job of my very own.

I asked Dad to loan me twenty cents to ride the streetcar. We never asked for money, it was always a loan, something you were always expected to pay back. I rode the streetcar across the Missouri River Bridge and in to Omaha. It was ten cents each way.

When I went to apply for the job at the Tip Top Curler Factory, the man took one look at me and grinned, "Honey, you're too young to work here, you have to be at least eighteen." "Good, because I'm nineteen," I said proudly. He told me I was going to have to prove it. I wish I had a picture of me that day. Looking back I bet I did look like I was about fourteen. He told me if I could bring back proof that I was nineteen, I could have the job. I went home and got my birth certificate. I got the job. Boy was Dad surprised. It was hard to get a job outside of the W.P.A. Now this meant someone would have to run the store and take care of Grandma. I was sorry I left Grandma. I talked to her and explained that I needed a life of my own. I was so happy when she told me she understood and wished me well. With no one there to take care of her they had no other choice and ended up putting Grandma in a home. I visited her there as often as I could. She was always happy to see me and never made me feel bad. Part of me felt like I deserted her but she never made me feel like that. I loved her very much.

I enjoyed my job at the curler factory. I had a very nice boss. His name was Mr. Schrom.

I worked right alongside three other men and Mr. Schrom always made sure that no one bothered me in any way. Matter of fact, I was the only female in that part of the factory.

I will always appreciate how Mr. Schrom and my foreman George Kendell looked out for me. I always did my part. Working on the assembly line was an endless job but I stayed trim. With all that bending and moving I had a built-in exercise program.

Laura Elizabeth Van Bibber 1947

CHAPTER 5

▼

Betty's son Johnny was born in 1944. This year was another turning point in my life. After only a few months working at the curler factory I was able to move away from home. I rented a room in a place in Omaha. For $3.50 a week I got a room, one meal a day and I could wash my clothes. I made $53 dollars for two weeks pay at my job. Pretty good money for me, or anyone else my age for that matter. Each week I received a little brown envelope with $53 dollars in cash. I was not a spender so I saved my money. Boy had my life changed in such a little period of time. Then came the biggest change of all, I met my first husband Ed. My boss warned me that he was not the right man for me but when you're in love, you don't hear anything. Ed was a very handsome man and he was very persuasive. I was twenty years old and I wanted a family of my own. Dad tried to talk me out of marrying Ed too. I married Ed.

I saved enough money to buy my wedding gown. His mom and dad put on the reception. Dad didn't go to my wedding but Mom, Warren and Mrs. Keeley came. Dad was very generous though. He provided us with all the household items a new couple needs; a stove, refrigerator, ringer washer, living room, dining room and bedroom furniture. Dad provided me with everything I needed to set up my new home, everything but the knowledge of what was expected of a new bride. Well, I can't blame that on Dad, Mom should have been the one to tell me about, well you know, the birds and the bees. I didn't know a thing. Can you believe it? I was twenty years old and had never even been kissed before. You can imagine the surprise I was in for on my wedding night. It was actually rather horrifying. Talk about a sheltered childhood. I wasn't allowed to talk or even hear about such things. My husband knew I was a virgin but I didn't even know what virgin meant. I never let on to him just how in the dark I was.

In 1946, in Omaha, Nebraska, my first baby Shirley Louise was born. I remember it like it was yesterday. It was Thanksgiving Day, on Thursday right at noon. It actually was one of the coldest days of the year but I was in seventh heaven. I thought I could never love another baby like I loved Shirley, even though I loved little Bobby with all my heart. Shirley was on her feet early, walking at nine months gave me all the exercise I needed to get back my girlish figure in no time. When I found out I had another baby on the way already I wasted no time in getting her potty trained. Fortunately for me, she learned very fast. How full of life she was. I wasn't disappointed in the least to find I was expecting another child because that was one of my biggest dreams, having a home full of children. I did a lot of sewing back then and little Shirley was right by my side. She had her little nose in every project I undertook at the sewing machine. She loved the idea that you could actually sew your own clothes just how you wanted them. I remember she told me once that when she grew up she was going to have her own dress shop.

Things went from wonderful to horrible. Ed started drinking quite a bit and sometimes he stayed out all night. He could not handle being a family man. Everything was rationed then; meat, gas, sugar. We were given tokens. Each family received so many, according to the number of people in their household. Everything was hard to get. We took the streetcar everywhere. I could not find a babysitter so going to work was out of the question for me. I did not know where to turn. Neither my parents nor my in-laws would help me. My parents pretty much told me that I made my own bed and my in-laws refused to admit that their son was being irresponsible. I had no other choice but to stay with Ed and hope for the best. I was strong, but I was going to have to be a lot stronger to take care of myself, my baby and a wayward husband. I tried very hard to please him. I would make special meals for him, kept the house extra nice but nothing worked. Matter of fact, things got worse. He stayed away longer and longer. Then when he did come home, he would be drunk. I wondered what happened to my marriage. What could I do fix this mess of a marriage I was in? What did I do? I was convinced it must be my fault.

Warren and the love of his life Mary Ann, were going to get married. They met at a Canteen Dance. It was love at first sight.

Warren served two years in the Marines as an MP. He was a good one. Warren asked Mary Ann to marry him when he was nineteen and she was seventeen. Shortly before they were married Mary Ann was diagnosed with cancer and had only a short time to live. They were both so very much in love they decided to proceed with the wedding plans. They were married on Sunday and she died on Wednesday. I was not there to help him. I know how hard it was for him. I was having so many problems with Ed though. I tried very hard to keep it quite.

In 1947 Teddy married Roy and Betty had a girl, Kathy. President Roosevelt died and Vice President Truman became President. In 1948, also in Omaha, my little Diana Jean was born. It was Sunday. The snow was coming down and the ground was very icy. I remember carrying her out of the hospital so gingerly, afraid she might break if I slipped on the icy ground. What a tiny baby. She weighed six pounds at birth and started to loose weight as soon as we brought her home. The doctor said she probably would not live past one year. When little Diana and I came home from the hospital I couldn't believe my eyes. Ed had sold our dining room set, and the big mirror we had was broken in pieces on the floor. I guess he had a party while I was in the hospital, with girls and all! I moved back home but I didn't stay long. My parents said that when you marry, you marry for life and send me back to Ed. I had no choice. Ed could not afford a decent place for us to live so we ended up in a little house that didn't even have an inside toilet. We had to use an outhouse out back. And here I was with two little girls. Diana was very frail too. She could not hold down milk. I put my main focus on my children at that time. Ed was just there … sometimes. Ed worked from job to job which provided us with barely enough to live on but I seemed to manage. I was desperate to find something to nourish my little Diana. She was failing right before my eyes. I prayed hard for her life and my prayers were answered. The good Lord led me to Ovaltine. I was always looking for something to help her and one day when I was in the store there was Ovaltine staring me right in the face. Something made me buy a jar and put it in her milk. She loved it and for some reason, it helped her hold the milk down. What a blessing. She was three months old then. From then on I kept the good Lord in my life. I could handle anything in my path from now on. Diana progressed rapidly. By the time she was a year old she was talking like she was two. She was still very tiny but what a little trooper. She was smart as a whip and since she was so tiny, that amazed people even more to hear this petite little girl carrying on a conversation before she was even walking. I remember being amazed at the different likes and dislikes of my two little girls. Diana wasn't really interested in sewing, she liked to be outside. If I was outside sweeping the porch or planting some flowers Diana was right there. She enjoyed being outside in the yard.

My little sister Teddy had a baby girl, Kathie. By this time, Teddy had left Roy and was on her own with her baby Kathie. I wondered why my parents never urged her to stay with her husband. I should have followed her lead. I was babysitting to earn extra money to help us out.

My father-in-law came over to tell me one of my brothers was killed in California. I had two brothers in California, Al and Warren. What a trauma that was. Either way it was going to be devastating. It was Al. Apparently he was in a car with some friends and they were going way to fast and hit a train. Al was killed instantly. That was the worst thing that ever happened in our family up until then. My heart sank very low.

The next day, while I was still trying to deal with the shock of losing my brother, two of Ed's brothers Jim and Ralph came over and told me he had some bar bills that needed to be paid. Right! As if I should be responsible for that. I said, "Oh sure, I'll get right down there and pay that tomorrow." Then I closed the door. I never talked to them again.

Lela and Harold brought Al's body back to Nebraska. He was buried in Omaha, next to Grandpa and little Bonnie Lou. That same year Betty had a boy and named him Dicky.

Everything was tumbling down on me. I had to do something or I was going to go crazy. I just couldn't go on like this. I had a wayward husband, two little girls and I was eight months pregnant with my third child. I had to get away from Ed somehow. Each time he left I hoped and prayed he would just stay gone, but he always came back and I always let him in. I finally got brave enough to tell him I didn't want to be his wife anymore. I talked to Lela about it and she told me to come out to California and that she and Harold would help me out with the kids and with whatever else I needed.

The next day when Ed left the house I called a used furniture man. He bought everything I had, including the kids' toys. I sold everything. I had enough to buy us bus tickets and a little left over to take care of me and the kids for a while. I thought I was going to make a clean get-a-way because Ed was usually gone at least a few days but this time, as we were getting ready to leave the house, he showed up. He looked around and saw that the only thing left in the house were his things. He threw a few of his belongings in a bag and jumped in the taxi with us. I didn't know what I was going to do. He boarded the bus with us. We weren't five miles down the road and he pulled out this bottle of whiskey. At the first stop the bus driver came back and took the bottle away from him. He told him, "When you're on my bus, you don't drink and you help take care of your family."

In 1949 we arrived in Hayward, California on July 4th. It was 9:30 at night and boy was it cold. Shirley and Diana were in these thin little sun suits and they were freezing. I had always thought California was warm. I gathered all the baby blankets I had and wrapped them up to keep them warm. We waited at the bus station until 10:30 and then I called a taxi and went to her home. When we arrived at Lela's it must have been about 2:00 AM. Evelyn, Nori and Howard were there and happy to see us. Evelyn made us some coffee and hot cocoa for the kids. Lela and Harold showed up later. They were surprised to see Ed with me. I explained to Lela what happened. She told me not to worry.

I was happy I could go to Howard's grade school graduation. This was the first graduation I attended other than my own. It sure made me feel good to be there.

Laura Elizabeth Van Bibber-Feise
1951

CHAPTER 6

▼

On August 22, 1949 in Hayward, California I gave birth to my third child, a little boy. I named him Edward Bernard. That was quite a big name for such a little guy. What a tiny baby he was. Lela had a box with HORSE MEAT written on it. I put a pillow in it and that was Eddie's first bed. I was glad when a friend of Lela's gave me a bassinet. Eddie must have heard us relate that story many times but he had his own version. Eddie always told everyone he came from a Kellogg's box. Well, he was mama's little prize. What an adorable little boy he was. He had dark, curly hair, big brown eyes and the most beautiful long eyelashes. He was a real boy though. Eddie liked to tinker. Give him some tools and he would be happy for hours. Ed named Eddie after him. I don't know why I let him. But then, I don't know why I let him follow us out to California. I was moving there to get away from him. I guess something inside me always hoped he would change. I loved him very much a long time ago. We never had much of a marriage from then on. He was just there once in awhile. Lela did what she could to help me. It was too much for her. She didn't know how to make Ed stay away either, he was always needing help.

I moved to a place that had little cabins. The rent was ten dollars a week. There were about fifteen cabins there. Some of the people that worked needed help with their washing and ironing and that was an easy way for me to support my kids and stay home with them at the same time. Ed was in and out. I didn't want him there but he had no place to go. There was a couple that lived a couple cabins down from me. When the husband would go to work, my husband would go over and spend the day with his wife. She always had a gallon of wine and they would drink all day. Then he would come home. Can you believe I put up with this? I felt sorry for him. He never beat me up or abused me in that way. If he did, it would have been a lot easier for me to get rid of him. I wouldn't have put up with that. But look at what I did put up with!

The day finally came though. I told him that he and his friend Mr. Whiskey were going to have to go. I had just had enough. This is when he told me I was his second choice anyway. He told me all about this girl named Ruth that he loved so much and wanted to marry but she wouldn't marry him. When he met me he thought it would work. He drank to forget about Ruth but never did. What a shame. I put up with his ways for all those years because I was told when you marry you do all you can to make your marriage work. All those years of torment, at least I got three beautiful children out of it. I can't put all the blame on him though. I was stupid enough to put up with his cheating and lying and take him back all those times. It's strange though. Even though it was the right thing to do and it had been a long time coming, I still had mixed emotions. I think it was more pity than love that kept me clinging to him for so long. Even when I found out I was his second choice I felt sorrier for him than I did for myself. Even though I was on my own with three little kids I was much better off. I could take care of my children but I couldn't take care of Ed anymore. The landlord had a son named Donald. He and Ed took off for Washington. I started a divorce. When he came back a few months later he wanted to try again. By this time I was much stronger. I told him, "Nope, too late, bye-bye." Poor Ed never even knew his children and they never knew him. Unfortunate but that was the way he chose to be. Things got a little rough there for a while. He would get drunk and bang on the door in the middle of the night. I finally ended up getting a restraining order to keep him away. Well, we all choose our own paths.

CHAPTER 7

▼

Just before my divorce was final I met the landlord of the cabins I was staying in. Oh I had met him before but it was different now. He kind of started calling on me, helping me. Even though he was fourteen years my senior he was quite a looker. To top it all off he was a real gentleman. I'll never forget the time I came home and found a big bag of groceries on my porch. Slowly but surely we started dating. We got the entire complex talking. My divorce wasn't quite final so they really thought they had something to talk about. I didn't care. We kept it cool enough for me to feel respectable. His name was Arthur or Art but I nicknamed him Arch. I remember Lela called him Auchie. He really swept me off my feet. As soon as my divorce was final we went to Reno and got married. He was quite a big spender too. I'll never forget the ring he bought me. It was so big I didn't even feel comfortable wearing it. I actually asked him to take it back and get me something smaller. He agreed, but he wanted me to use the money that was left over to buy something that I wanted or needed. Not only did I get a nice ring but also I had a ball shopping for the kids. Besides the new clothes I got them, I remember buying the girls a new, almost life-size doll. You should have seen their faces. I don't know who was more filled with joy, them or me. Arch was happy I was so tickled about shopping for the kids but I think he really wanted me to spend the money on myself. He took care of that though. That Christmas he showered us all with gifts. Among the many other things I got a beautiful set of dishes, a gleaming new set of silverware and a brand new sewing machine.

My whole life changed. Not only did I get a wonderful husband who loved me dearly and treated me with respect, he also loved my children and helped me care for them as if they were his own. I also became a stepmother. Arch had two sons,

Eugene and Donald, better known as Gene and Don. It was a bit strange being their step mom at first because they were only a few years younger than me! I couldn't have asked for better stepchildren. They were very nice young men, more like my friends and still are to this day.

My little Eddie was still walking around with his bottle. One day Arch told him, "You're a big boy now, you don't need that bottle. Why don't you just throw it away?" Eddie walked right over to the trashcan and threw his bottle away. I just loved how Arch interacted with the kids. One time Arch's dad came to visit. Shirley and Diana found their new Grandpa's plug of tobacco. They thought it was candy. I guess you could say they both bit off more than they could chew. Both of them got sicker than dogs. Arch felt real bad about that.

Donald went into the Army. He fought in the Korean War and then was stationed in Alaska for two years. Arch was a carpenter. This was when I learned to love to work with tools. In fact, I helped him work on projects here and there, more as the years went by. I became a very good helper. I could lay shingles as fast or faster than any man he had working for him. I was proud of that. I helped Arch built two duplexes behind our home in Happy Land. There were a lot of service men in the area so they were always rented. That was actually the name of the street where we lived, Happy Land. It really was Happy Land for me too. My children were happy, well-fed, nice clothes. There was no fighting, arguing, drinking and carrying on. I finally had what I really wanted, a happy, wonderful marriage.

Things were going great until the day I got the news that Grandma died. I had not seen her for three years but wrote to her often. She was seventy-two. Grandma actually lived a long time for the condition she was in.

On October 27, 1951, my fourth child arrived. Arch and I had our first child together. We had a little girl and named her Arlene Elizabeth. We were so happy with our little girl. She was quite a Daddy's girl too. When Arch would go to work Arlene would not eat and would cry most of the time he was gone. I told my concern to the doctor. He told me not to worry and that she wouldn't starve. He assured me she would eat when she got hungry. With the help of her two sisters and brother Arlene talked at a very early age. In fact, I had to keep my eye on her, she would talk to anyone. She was very outgoing, not shy one bit and as she grew she found that she could be entertaining and make people laugh. She was quick to memorize any story I would tell her a few times and she even tried to copy the different voices I would use for the different characters in the story.

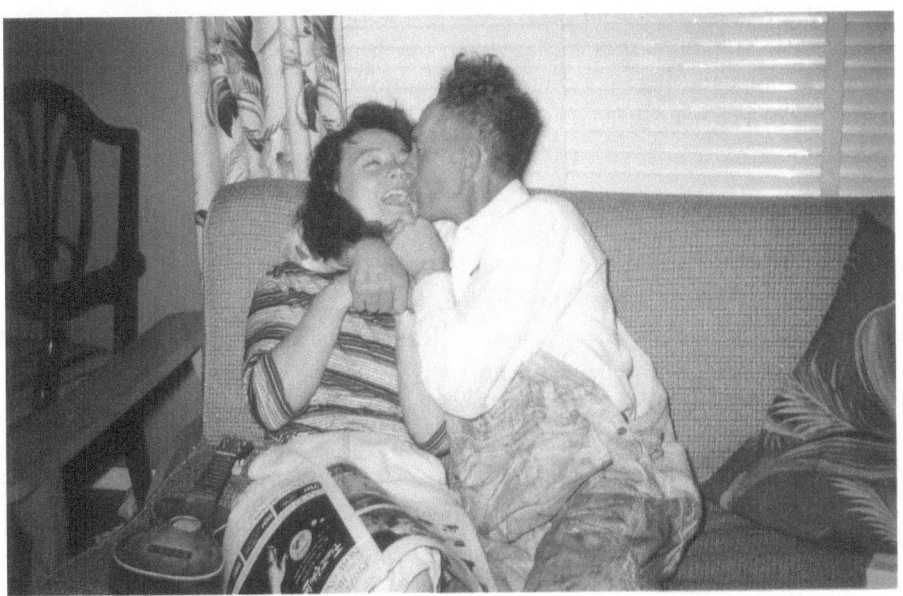

Laura Elizabeth Feise & Arthur Theodore Feise 1951

To me, my family was just the right size now. After all, with Gene, Don, Shirley, Diana, Eddie, and Arlene we had six children. That was plenty enough for any couple to rear. Thank goodness I loved to cook, clean and iron because I had plenty of it to do. Actually ironing was my favorite. I could stand in my living room and either listen to the radio and sing or watch my favorite soaps on T.V. and iron for hours. I even took in ironing from other people and made extra money.

In 1952 we moved to Hayward. The house was bigger and it was nice to have a little more room, at least that's what I thought. Not long after we moved in Art's brother Gordon and his wife Myrtle moved in with us. I was pregnant, again and Myrtle was expecting twins. Art was always trying to help some one out, unfortunately even at the expense of his own family. Here I had four kids and doing most of the work around the house because Myrtle was pregnant and not much help. What a trial that was. Our neat little organized household became a discombobulated mess. Cooking meals and washing clothes were no longer fun things on my list, just an endless chore from morning until night. I actually asked them to leave once but they told me they had nowhere to go. One day I just had enough. I told Arch I was not going to cook another meal or wash another dish as long as they remained in our household. I went to the store and bought bologna and bread. I came home, bundled up the kids, and took them to the park. For the next three days we went to the park at dinnertime and had our sandwiches. Arch went with us but he wasn't happy about it. Soon Gordon and Myrtle grew tired of fending for them selves and moved out. Sad to say, all they did was find another family member to move in with. Art's brother Louie was the unlucky recipient of Gordon, Myrtle and her two new babies. Myrtle had twin boys, Ricky and Randy. They now had six kids, Carol, Dale, Ronny, and Sharon, who they nicknamed Peachy, Ricky and Randy. Carol and Dale had already left home when Gordon and Myrtle came to live with us. I'll tell you, my group didn't seem quite so big after they left. What a relief. Little did I know this was only the beginning in a long line of extra family members finding shelter at our home. It wouldn't have been so bad if when they came they contributed in some way but most didn't. I could never make Arch understand that I enjoyed helping others too but when you see that they are using you it's time to show them the door.

Arthur Theodore Feise & Arlene Elizabeth Feise 1951

CHAPTER 8

▼

We sold our home in Hayward and moved to a big two-story house in Pleasanton. There were nine cabins out back. Art and I remodeled them and rented them out.

In 1953 Gene married a lovely girl named Delores. They both worked for Southern Pacific Railroad. On June 16, 1953 my fifth child arrived, our daughter June Marie was born. I guess you can figure out where I got that name. June was adorable. She was an extremely happy baby with cute little red cheeks. We called her June Bug. At a very young age June was extremely particular about what she wore and what she ate. If I ever gave her something she didn't want to eat she would just hold her breath. This was so troubling to me because not only did it scare me, but she always got her way because of it. She was a smart little thing. June was very fussy about the clothes she wore too. If I started to dress her in something she didn't want to wear I had a battle on my hands. When she was about a year old she let me know she didn't want that bottle anymore. I walked by her crib and she threw it at me, hit me right in the head. She thought that was pretty funny. Actually, I did too. I got the message though. I guess that's the way it is. Sometimes you just don't get it until you're hit on the head. Despite her insistent attitude June was easy to care for. A joyful baby. I'll never forget how she used to like to do the Twist like Chubby Checkers. She could really dance. June was very independent. She would be happy to entertain herself but really never got the chance with so many brothers and sisters around. She wanted things her way though. She had definite ideas about how things should be done.

In 1954 Donald went to work in Auburn. The job didn't last long so he decided to come back home, but we weren't there. It was quite a surprise for

Donald when he climbed in the window and found an empty house. We had moved to Aptos, a little town outside of Santa Cruz. The place we bought not only had a home for us but it had a small grocery store, a bar and ten cabins. The place we bought was called Glen Echo. We were really busy there. Arch made some changes to the place right away. He made a small lunch counter, enlarged the bar and took out the grocery store. We were only there a short while when we experienced something I had always heard that California was famous for, an earthquake. The mirror in the living room was swaying. I thought it was the kids jumping on the bed or something. Then the floor started rolling. Bottles rolled off the shelf and busted all over the floor. It was a mess. Just a week before a government official came to our bar and took all the Hadacol off the shelf. I think it was about ninety percent alcohol.

Gene and Delores lived in San Francisco. It wasn't too far away and we saw them often. Delores and I became good friends. In 1954 they had their first baby, a little girl named Joanne. She was our first grandchild. Donald became a surveyor and moved to San Jose. Arch took care of the bar. The rest was mine, with five baby chicks trailing behind me where ever I went. I truly loved it with my children close by me; just like an old mother hen. I really was strict, I had to be. I had so much to do and I needed them to behave and listen. They did too. Everyone noticed how well behaved they were and that made me very proud, of them and myself. The kids pretty much never left my sight. There was this one-day I got quite a scare. All the kids were taking a nap. Arlene woke up and went to one of the other cabins where a little friend of hers lived. I was frantic. The lady brought her home, she was only two.

I got a letter from my brother Warren. He was getting married to a woman named Jean. He sounded very happy. Gordon and Myrtle moved into two of our cabins with all their children. They lived there rent-free and ate in the café. Arch was on another crusade. I can't believe it happened again but it did. But that wasn't all. I was pregnant again. Maybe that was just the news I needed to put me over the edge again. It was costing us a fortune to feed all of them. Gordon was working at the San Mateo dump. It wasn't like they didn't have money to live on.

Lela and Harold moved into one of our cabins with there daughters Evelyn and Nori. I welcomed them. At last, I had some help. Howard was in the Navy. We would have free special spaghetti feeds with salad and French bread once in a while to bring in the customers. I thought Arch was crazy at first but boy did we sell the beer. Local officials didn't like us giving away free food for some reason so we ended up charging thirty-five cents a plate. Our business was thriving.

We had dances ever Friday night. Don and Gene and a friend of theirs played music. Lela and I cooked all the food, Arch and Harold and a friend tended the bar.

On October 25, 1954 my sixth child came on the scene, our little Teddy was born. We named him Alan Theodore but we always called him Ted. He was so cute. Little redheaded, freckled face Teddy was so adorable. He loved playing in the dirt outside and joining in with the singing inside. I remember one time when he was about five, Arlene June and Ted set up some chairs in the dining room and gave the whole family a talent show. June and Arlene sang and Ted was playing the guitar. Well, his guitar was the little shovel from the fireplace but he sure could play. He really got into it. What a little show they put on.

There was always something happening at Glen Echo. Another government official came and busted up our pinball machine. He said it was gambling, and gambling was against the law. They busted them up all over town. Too bad too, the proceeds from that machine paid our electric bill every month. Eventually the whole lifestyle got a bit too much for us and we put Glen Echo up for sale. Harold got a job in Hayward so he and Lela moved there. Myrtle and Gordon moved to Auburn and just left their two oldest boys, Dale and Ronny with us. They were going to help Arch build our new home on some property we bought in Rio Del Mar just south of Santa Cruz. That lasted for about three months. We took them home. They just couldn't understand why they couldn't stay. They didn't realize they were more of a burden than they ever were of any help. We were very close to the Santa Cruz Boardwalk. We took the kids there a lot. Our place was right on the golf course. We paid five hundred dollars for that lot, fifteen dollars a month. I wish we had it now. I'm sure it's priced in the millions by now.

Eddie used to hide out in the Eucalyptus trees just off our back yard and get the stray golf balls. Then he would sell them back to the golfers.

In 1955 Donald married my sister Lela's daughter Elnora. Lela's other daughter Evelyn married Clive in a double wedding. That same year Gene and Delores had their second baby; a little girl named Linda. We were a very close family, always getting together for one reason or another or for no reason at all. Whenever Lela and Harold came to visit Teddy was always at Harold's side. Ted loved Uncle Harold. So much went on between 1955 and 1957. We lived in the house we were building for three months with no power or water. I cooked on a woodstove. We were the first people on the block in that subdivision. If you go there today you can't see any open space at all, it's just one house after another, after another. Washing dirty diapers in a bucket was one chore I was glad to leave behind once the electric finally got to our house. We celebrated that night with a big dinner and toasted the occasion with milk all around.

In 1957 Gene and Delores had a baby boy. The named him James but every-one always called him Jimmy. He was a little premature but he got along just fine. Oh yeah, surprise, I was pregnant again. This was actually the first time I remember being unhappy about being pregnant. That didn't last long though. On June 21, 1957 I gave birth to my seventh child, a little girl, Lorraine May. We always called her Lorrie though and she was beautiful. No one could take her away from me, she was mine. She was a calm easy going baby. Lela, Harold and Arch took me to the hospital. They went for coffee and by the time they came back Lorrie was born. Nori came to the hospital with Arch to pick us up. She bought Lorrie a pretty pink bonnet and a sweater to wear home. She also had made a complete dinner for the whole family so I wouldn't have to cook. I was very grateful for her thoughtfulness. I couldn't ask for a kinder niece or daugh-ter-in-law, she just happened to be both as it turns out. What a joy she was to me. Just as all my other children before had their particular interests so did Lorrie. If I was in the kitchen, Lorrie was in the kitchen. She loved to help me cook, or bake or anything else I just happened to be doing in the kitchen. I just knew she would turn out to me my little homemaker.

Warren and Jean had their first baby, a girl, Jolene. Donald and Nori were building a home two blocks from us on Rio Del Mar. We all went out for a movie once in awhile. We would go to the drive-in theater on Saturday nights. I made Kool-Aid and popcorn. My kids never knew what a Coke was. I remember once we were watching a cowboy movie. The horses went off the screen and Arlene wanted to know where they went. We all got a laugh out of that one. They all came up with funny stuff. I wish I had written them all down.

A few times Joanne, Linda and Jimmy would come and stay with us for a few days. They were good little children. They fit right in with all of mine.

Little Joanne was always coming up with things too. One day we were all going to the store and we pulled up along side a group of guys on motorcycles. Joanne looks at them and then yells to me, "Peel out Gramma!" We all got a kick out of that. Linda was the sweetest little girl. She was very shy and polite. I loved being a Grandma. The best part was that you could love them to pieces then send them home. After all, babies were my life.

*Ludwig Feise, Lela Cunningham, two cousins, Art Feise, Elnora Cunningham-Feise,
Laura Feise (holding Teddy) Minnie Feise, Harold Cunningham, Shirley Roza-Feise,
Arlene Feise, cousin, June Feise, Diana Roza-Feise, Edward Roza-Feise, cousin*
1955

Laura Elizabeth Feise, Arthur Theodore Feise, and Alan Theodore Feise Hayward,
CA, Foothill Blvd
1955

Nori and Donald moved to Red Bluff. Donald was a surveyor for the Diamond Match Company. We were looking for property in Red Bluff, or Redding. We found a small house on forty acres in Flournoy, about forty miles southwest of Red Bluff. It was beautiful, everything was green, at least in the spring that is.

There was a little old house that had three bedrooms, one bath and a porch that went around half of the house. It was furnished with some old furniture, a wood stove in the kitchen and a fireplace. Arch and I both loved it. We knew it could use some fixing up but it would be a great place to raise the kids. They wanted forty-five hundred dollars for it. For a deposit of twenty dollars it was ours. We sold our home and moved to Flournoy. It was our little ranch. That ranch today is worth a couple million dollars.

The day we moved in our new neighbors met us at the gate; Elwyn, Darlene and their son Bobby. We had to cross two creeks to get to our place. We got stuck in the creek on the next day, truck, trailer and all. Eddie went for help and

Elwyn came and pulled us out with his tractor. He was always there when we needed him. What a delight to see our new place. When we stopped Shirley, Diana, Eddie, Arlene, June and Teddy all took off every which way, exploring their new home. There was forty acres to run wild. It took three days to unload and get everything situated. The house was pretty small so we had some arranging to do. Since there were only three bedrooms, the first one was for Arch and I. We screened in the porch and put the girls out there. Ed and Ted got one of the bedrooms. Arch's mother died so the other bedroom ended up as a guest bedroom for Arch's Dad. Before his mother died she asked me if I would name one of my kids after her. Since her name was Minnie Bertha I just couldn't do that to Lorrie. I remember how much my sister Betty hated her name Bessie.

Diana Feise, Linda Feise, Shirley Feise, June Feise, Ted Feise, Joanne Feise, Ed Feise
Flournoy, CA 1959

When we moved in it was April. Everything was green, and the creek was running right behind the house. There were all kinds of wildlife out there; deer, geese, ducks and rattlesnakes. With all the snakes we ended up finding, none of the kids ever were hurt by them. What a joy the ranch was. Arch bought three horses. Their names were Socks, a beautiful Sorrel stallion and two mares, Monica and Lady. None of us had ever ridden a horse before except for Arch but we all caught on right quick. We had a milk cow, chickens, three sows, twelve geese, and three dogs: Lucky, Penny and Yega, and two cats. To this day I can't believe we never planted a garden. Elwyn had a hog named Elvis. We let Elvis come over to visit our sows and it wasn't long before we had a bunch of little piggies. What a sight to see; seven little kids sitting on the fence watching the little pigs being born. Every time one was born they would all cheer. It was so fun watching them get so excited. There was one little runt and Eddie really wanted to take care of him all by himself. We let him. The runt grew up to be one of the biggest pigs we had. I think that was because that little pig loved creamed corn, but then, that was their main dish.

Arch's brother Gordon was the caretaker for the San Mateo City Dump at that time. We used to get all kinds of stuff from the dump, lumber, toys, clothes and yes sometimes-even food. One time a warehouse caught on fire and all the stuff in the warehouse went to the dump. Gordon called Arch and told him to come and look to see if there was anything he wanted. Arch brought home, among other items, cases and cases of cream corn. We put up a can opener out at the pigpen and fed all the corn to the pigs. They loved it. All the kids had likes and dislikes but none of them liked cream corn after that.

Diana hated spinach and Eddie hated peas. Whenever we had spinach Diana's cheeks would be so full of spinach it looked like she was going to pop. She just couldn't swallow it. It made her gag. Eddie would line the bottom of his plate with his peas and make us think he ate them. Eddie always had a big glass of water with his meal. It seemed as though he had a lot of trouble swallowing but the doctor told me there was nothing wrong with his throat. Years later we found out there was something wrong and he went through a very serious operation to correct it. The rest of the kids ate everything I put on their plate. Shirley, Diana and Eddie all loved to cook.

They all enjoyed being in the kitchen, trying to help in one way or another, with the cooking that is. Not too many of them liked doing the dishes but they all had to take their turns. Evenings were a fun time for us. We always sat down together to dinner. Shirley and Diana had the duty of doing the dishes until Arlene and June got old enough. After dinner we would all go in and watch TV. I would make cookies or cake or pie for dessert. One of Arch's favorite desserts was Tapioca pudding or bread pudding.

Shirley was very outgoing, always there to help. I depended on her a lot, probably too much at times. I worked out of the house a lot with Arch on different building projects and Shirley was always in charge. She grew up real fast.

Diana was quite and easy going, willing to do anything I asked. She was a very sweet natured child. Diana loved working in the yard then and still does today.

Diana's favorite song was "You Are My Sunshine."

Eddie was full of life, my little comedian. He could make all of us laugh. He was fun to be around. Arlene loved animals. She got a lamb from Elwyn for a pet. The ewe had abandoned it for some reason. She treasured that lamb. We build a little pen for it and fed it with a bottle. One night it was particularly cold and the lamb did not have sense enough to got inside the little shed and froze to death. Arlene was broken hearted. She was a sweet natured child. I remember when she first had to wear glasses, she hated it. The doctor told me she had amblyopia. She inherited the problem from her dad. She was quite a tomboy and went through pair after pair. She was the only one who ever had to continue wearing glasses on through to adulthood. Eddie and Shirley had to wear them for a while.

Each of the kids had their own little personalities. June was the one who loved babies. Whenever there was a baby around June wanted to hold it, feed it, take care of it if she could. I remember when June was about four she got up in the middle of the night and took Lorrie to bed with her. When I got up and found an empty bassinette you better believe I was frantic. Lights were going on all over the house and I was checking every room and every bed. Then I flipped on the light in the girl's room. There was little Lorrie lying across June's chest sound asleep. June didn't think she did anything wrong. She explained, "She was crying so I went and got her."

Teddy was very playful. He loved digging in the dirt. He loved animals, especially our horse Socks, but he never rode him. He was always saying something that came out of nowhere and made everyone laugh. One time we were coming into San Francisco on our way to visit Gene and Delores and Ted got a look at San Francisco Bay for the first time. His eyes got as big as saucers. "Look at the big reservoir!" he said in amazement. The biggest body of water he had seen up until that time was the reservoir on our forty acres in Flournoy. When he saw his first wrecking yard he was ready to go home because that was far too many smashed cars in one spot for him. Lorrie was very mellow. She had a cat that was almost as big as she was and she used to carry around by the neck all over the place. Sometimes I thought she was going to choke that cat to death but he always came back for more. We had a little Cocker Spaniel named Penny that used to follow Lorrie around where ever she went too. One day when we went came home from a day of shopping in town; little Penny was lying on the porch with a hurt paw. I think the poor little thing got it caught in a trap or something. The next day Penny died. We buried her up by the front gate. The same place we buried Lucky. Lucky was a beautiful Irish Setter. He was Arch's dog before we got married but he soon became a family favorite. Lucky loved everyone and everyone loved Lucky.

In 1959 Warren and Jean had another girl and named her Shelly. Howard married Donna. Donna and I became good friends. She had a little girl named Beth. The girls loved it when they came out. I think Beth enjoyed her cousins too.

All the kids loved to sing, so did I. I used to wake them up in the mornings by turning on the radio and singing, while I was making breakfast and getting their lunches ready for school. I was their alarm clock. A familiar phase around our house was, "Get your coats, the bus is leaving." Whoever stayed home had to work so most of the time everyone was out the door and ready for school. When they got a little bigger they walked to school or rode their bikes.

I was pretty strict with the kids, I had to be. When you have that many they could just plow right over you if you let it get out of hand. It worked though.

None of the kids ever talked back to me. They always listened and for the most part were very well behaved. I'm sure they had a thing or two to say when they were only among themselves but they took care to not let me hear it if they did.

In 1960 Arch was always busy doing something around the ranch or working on a building project somewhere else. Elwyn raised sheep on his thousand acres right next to our forty acres. When Elwyn sheared the sheep in the spring the kids used to like to watch. What a site to see. There were mounds and mounds of fluffy white cotton everywhere.

We always had company out at the ranch. I remember one time when Gene and Delores' three; Joanne, Linda and Jimmy came for a visit. One day little Jimmy got up early all by himself. I heard a noise and got up to find little Jimmy in the sink. He had some bread and Grandpa's pills. I was so scared. I didn't know if he took any and he was too little to tell me so I took him to the doctor. The doctor assured me that if he would have taken any of the pills he would have showed some signs by now so we took him home. We went about our usual day, working on the house, kids playing outside. Later that day I noticed Jimmy's face was bright red. Still worried about the pills I took Jimmy back to the doctor. The doctor asked, "How many kids did you say you had?" When I told him he said, "And you don't know what a sun burn looks like?" Oh well, better safe than sorry. Jimmy was so full of life, not afraid of anything. We had a creek right behind the house. He went swimming right along with the rest of the kids. He would jump right in with no fear and he was only three.

When Donald, Nori, Gene and Delores came a fun time was had by all. Gene and Don would bring their musical instruments out and play music and sing. Arch was very musically inclined. He could play the mandolin, the violin, the accordion and he could sing. I remember little Teddy joining in singing and playing his little broom guitar. Later we bought Teddy a guitar of his own. The girls learned to sing. Shirley and Diana taught Arlene and June how to harmonize and they all sang rather well together. They sang together at school and at church. One time I dressed them all in matching outfits and they sang for this talent show at school. We called them The Feise Five; Shirley, Diana, Arlene, June and Lorrie.

The Feise's
Gene, Art, Don, Shirley, Laura, Diana, Ed, Arlene, June, Ted, Lorrie
(I thought I was finished but Elaine wasn't born yet)
1960

CHAPTER 9

▼

There was always something happening out at the ranch. One day Elwyn and Darlene's son Bobby was riding his pony when a rattlesnake bit the pony's leg. Bobby was thrown to the ground but not hurt. Arch and Elwyn rushed the pony to the vet but it didn't make it. There were a lot of rattlesnakes on the ranch. They were the pits among the cherries. That's what they geese came in good for. They kept the snakes at a safe distance from the kids. I don't know how the kids all escaped from being bit. They were all over that ranch. They were the cherries among the pits. Speaking of pits, did I say we had a lot of company? Much of the time it was welcome, they helped and we had a bunch of fun. That was until Gordon and Myrtle showed up again. This time they asked if we would take care of their wayward son Ronny because they couldn't manage him. As if we could? I guess they thought he couldn't get into any trouble way out there in the sticks. They never even considered what a handful he would be for us. Did I say us? I should have said me. Arch told Gordon Ronny could stay and he would put him to work. Right! Not only did Gordon leave Ronny with us he also left us with a quarter horse that wasn't broke and no one could ride him. Buckels was his name. Evelyn's husband Clive came the closest to ridding him but he even got bucked off several times.

That next year was awful. Ronny was a terror. The schoolteacher, Mr. Shrum told me to send Ronny home. He thought Ronnie was a bad influence on the kids. He was right. Arch thought I just wasn't being fair to him and I should try harder.

Arch always wanted to help someone else, sometimes more than his own kids. Sorry, I loved Arch but that was the truth. He always wanted to help the underdog, but he didn't realize I was the underdog. I wished he had as much understanding and patience with his own children. Arch was not only short on patience but his disciplinary skills were terrible. Arch was not the best person with children. The way he disciplined the children was hard for me because he always got his way. I realized later in life I could have done something about his actions. I guess that is why today, no one gets mistreated around me. For the most part, I did do the best I could, and better. If I had it to do all over though I wouldn't let Arch impose his backward style of correction on the children and I would have stepped in and fixed it when it was happening. You can't go back though. You can only move forward. I hope my children will try to concentrate on the good I did for them instead of the mistakes I made. I loved my children with all my heart and to this day they are number one through ten in my life. I love you kids.

When Shirley was thirteen she graduated from the eighth grade. There were only seven in her graduating class. Did I mention that the kids went to a two-room schoolhouse? First grade though fourth grade in one room, fifth through eighth in the other. There were no school buses or school bells. Oh I take that back, the teacher did come out and ring a bell when it was time for them to come in from recess. A regular Little House On The Prairie.

About that same time Howard and Donna had a little girl and named her Kim. When Myrtle and Gordon came for a visit I had Ronny's bags packed and boy were they upset. They had brought Ronny a twenty-two rife to shoot on the ranch. Too bad, he was going. I told them "You can take that gun and Ronny home with you when you leave." I had had enough. I remember Gordon asking Arch, "Are you going to listen to her? Who's the man of this family anyway?" I had already told Arch I wasn't going to take care of Ronny anymore and if he wanted him to stay he could cook, clean and do his laundry for him. Ronny went home. Peace and quite for a while anyway, as much as one can have with seven children. Then Arch's father came to live with us. He was fine for a while, until he became irritated with me for giving more attention to my family than to him. He really had some strange ideas. He didn't believe it when the man landed on the moon, he thought it was fake. When Arch's father starting become more than we could handle, Arch's sister Emma said she would take care of him. He became a real pill for her too. The older he got the more attention he insisted on. I think he was suffering from Alzheimer's too but I didn't even know what that was then.

Next Arch's brother Louie came to stay with us for a while. He had heart problems. We took him to the hospital three times in two months. He finally moved back to the Bay Area so he could be closer to his doctor. He died a short time later.

Howard and Donna had a little boy, Jeffery.

Arthur Theodore Feise
1952

CHAPTER 10

▼

The next relative that came to stay with us was Arch's sister Julia, along with her husband Jim and their daughter Jenny. It was hard enough for us to manage with nine people in the house, add three more and that's the straw that breaks the camel's back. I never got any help from Julia either. I was expected to just cook, clean, and wash that much more and not complain. Eddie and Teddy ended up giving up their room to Julia and Jim and camped out in the living room. Jenny moved in with the girls. I never trusted Jim. He was sneaky and weird. Arch thought I was being over protective and had a wild imagination. Never the less, I told the girls to stay away from him and never be alone with him. I found out much later it was not the girls he bothered. Heaven only knows what I would have done if I would have found out then. Raising children is like not being able to see the forest for the trees. You think you are doing a good job by making sure they are not hungry or cold, that they have a clean home and decent clothes to wear. But there is so much more. You get so wrapped up in taking care of their physical needs you forget about your own needs. Sometimes you don't take enough time to pay attention to their emotional needs. It's so difficult when you have so many. I don't regret having so many children but I wish I would have had more time to spend with them one on one.

So much went on in our lives between 1960 and 1962. One morning I was fixing breakfast, Jim always had six eggs. I remember Julia saying to Jim, "When we get a place of our own you won't be having six eggs for breakfast." I couldn't help but answer, "So when is that going to be?" The heat was on then. She actually started complaining about the fact that I had started putting their laundry in a separate basket for her to do instead of washing their things right along with ours. I actually felt kind of sorry for Julia. She was a nice enough person. We ended up in a big shouting match and I told them it was time to leave. After all, they had been with us for over a year. True, Jim had been helping Arch but his assistance did not out weigh the problems and expenses I was contending with. Arch did not agree. He was fuming. He said he needed Jim's help. I always had to get to my wits end before I would stick up for what was right, my sanity. Why did I continue to agree every time one of Art's relatives showed up on our door-step? Like I said, I loved him but he could be very intimidating. The sad thing was, I liked helping people too, but it was always so much nicer when they chipped in. Oh, Julia did try some times. Once in a while she would cook a meal or sweep the floor. No body is perfect. Heaven only knows I wasn't but I was tired of being imposed upon.

Warren and Jean had another girl, Liza.

Nori, Evelyn and Howard were a big part of my life, a big wonderful part. When they were around it was like a breath of fresh air. They were like my own kids. I was always around them when they were growing up.

In 1961 some one called me from Omaha and told me that Ed, my first hus-band died of Cirrossis of the liver. No big surprise. He pickled himself in booze. What a wasted life, he was thirty-four. It seemed strange to even think he was my husband at one time.

Arch was building a huge shop behind the house. We had all the things we were buying here and there for the new house. I got my first new washer and dryer. What a blessing compared to that old wringer washer.

We had a goat named Abraham. He got that name because he was born on Lincoln's birthday. He followed us everywhere we went. One time he even climbed up in the rafters with us. He got in the house one time when we were all in town and left his little goat pellets on every bed in the house. I made sure I closed all the windows the next time we were leaving.

Arch was now on two projects that would keep him busy for a while.

He was building a house for Lela and Harold on some property they bought about a half a mile behind the school. At the same time, Arch started building our new home about five hundred yards from our old one. Lela and Harold bought all the lumber for our house for payment. We would all pitch in with what ever we could on either house.

Our beloved dog Lucky died on New Years Day. We buried him along side Penny up by the gate.

During deer season the weekends were busy around our house. Between our forty acres and Elwyn's thousand acres, we always had a place to hunt and everyone got a deer. Donald, Nori, Gene, Delores, Lela, Harold and their families would all come out. Early mornings you could see deer cross over on a ridge with a big buck in the lead.

We got another dog, Yega. She ended up having so many pups. One time she had her pups all over the ranch, thirteen of them. Shirley, Diana and Eddie went out and found them all and brought them to her.

The deer season thing really started to boomerang. Friends started showing up with their families and bringing friends of their own, many times without even asking. One time I had thirty people at my house. They camped all over; inside, outside, what a mess our house was in. We only had two bathrooms and that wasn't even enough for all the kids I had. Some people brought food but the only help I got cooking it was from Nori and Lela. They always tried to help but it was a losing battle most of the time. About the time the third year rolled around Nori and I got smart. We got ourselves a gun and went hunting with the guys. Arch had bought a couple of pistols that Gene put pearl handles on. Nori and I strapped them on. With pistols on our hips and rifles in our hands we looked like a couple of pistol packin' mamas. Big hunters we were. We wouldn't have shot a deer for anything. One time a big buck came out of the brush right in front of us. It was amazing to see a big animal like that so close. He turned and walked a way and so did we. It was a lot of fun though. I was so happy Lela stayed back at the house and looked after the kids. She told everyone else they had to fend for themselves. Lela taught me well. From then on I stopped being the hostess for all the company and things changed. People didn't come around as often after that. One time there was about twenty people showed up. I had two chickens and wondered how I was going to feed everyone. Lela, Nori and I peeled a bunch of carrots, potatoes and onions and made the two biggest potpies I ever saw. Everyone ate and enjoyed themselves for the weekend. I told them they had to let me know after this when they were coming up. I just couldn't handle so many people at one time. I am sure they thought I was being selfish, especially since we had so many deer on the property. I was glad to see them go. Well most of them anyway.

It was nice having just our little group; Gene, Delores, Donald, Nori, Lela, Harold, Howard, Donna, Evelyn and Clive and of course Elwyn and Darleen. There were a few other family members I enjoyed seeing but for the most part this was the regular group we enjoyed. Our evenings were full of music. Everyone played an instrument or joined in the singing. Arch wasn't too happy when the crowds started to thin though. He loved having lots of people around. I went hunting with Arch during the week. Lorrie went with us too. That kid could spot a deer a mile away. It was so cute how she would take her little hands and put them on my cheeks and show me where the deer were. Lorrie loved to hammer nails too. While the rest of the kids were in school and we were busy building the house Lorrie could sit for the longest time hammering nails into a piece of wood block. It was fun to watch her. She actually thought she was helping.

Sometimes on Saturdays we would take all of the kids to lunch in Corning. They got a coke, a hamburger and fries. What a treat. June would always want an Orange Crush, she didn't like Coke. The only drink they got at home was milk, Kool-Aid or hot chocolate.

Once in a while we would go to the drive-in theater. I would make big bags of popcorn and jugs of Kool-Aid. We always had a great time.

Sometimes Nori would take Shirley and Diana for a week at a time. Sometimes she would take Arlene and June. She even took all four of them once. She loved the kids and they loved her. Arlene and June stayed for almost the whole summer one time. They had a great time but I sure missed them. They used to stay at Gene and Delores too. I was so glad that all the kids got to grow up together.

The Feise's
Jimmy, Delores, Gene, Elnora, Don, Art, Laura, Shirley, Ed, Ted,
Linda, Joanne, Diana, Arlene, June, Lorrie
(Elaine still wasn't born yet)
1961

CHAPTER 11

▼

Have you ever had a tragedy, which was out-weighed by blessings? Well it happened to me the day our house burned down to the ground.

Arch was having a lot of back problems so we had been to the doctor quite a few times that year trying to figure out why. This one time in particular, Art and I were at the doctor in Corning. Except for Lorrie, all the kids were at home. I heard the fire truck scream by as I was sitting in the waiting room but I never imagined it was my home that was up in flames. A neighbor called the doctor's office and told us our house burned down but all our kids were okay. My mind went into a tailspin. That was the longest ride home I ever had in my whole life. Even though the neighbor told me that all the kids were okay, I still was worried. I prayed so hard all the way home. I was not sure if she was telling me the truth or not. I prayed she wasn't just sparing me some pain. When I got to Elwyn and Darlene's house there were the children, all safe and sound. Then we went out and took a look at our house. Everything was gone. The house was burned to the ground and all the items we were storing in the building behind the house were gone. All the things for our new home, the kids bikes, my new washer and dryer, all our clothes, dishes, bedding, furniture, everything was gone up in smoke. The most important thing was safe though, the kids. The fireman said the fire started from the dryer. As luck would have it, just less than a week before the fire a friend of ours, Mr. Tandy, who just happened to be an insurance salesman, told us we should get some insurance on our home. He tried to talk Arch into getting a policy for twenty thousand dollars coverage. Arch settled for fifteen. We were supposed to pay the premium on the policy that day that I took Arch to the doctor in corning but I forgot. It turns out, Mr. Tandy sent the policy in for us anyway.

When Mr. Tandy heard about the fire he was glad he sent it in for us. I never called it luck, I knew God was looking out for us, especially when none of my children were harmed by the fire. Darleen and Elwyn welcomed our whole family into there tiny home. We stayed there for a week.

The whole ordeal upset me quite a bit but I just turned it over to God. He says he will never let you go through anymore than you can handle so I know he helped me get through it. It really took a toll on Arch. He was pretty sick. All of our plumbing and electrical supplies for the new house were in the shed that went up in flames so we had to buy new stuff and start all over. That didn't do his ulcers on bit of good. All the lumber Harold had bought for our new home was gone too. When we finished purchasing all the things we needed for the new house that were destroyed we spent over sixty-five hundred dollars. Elwyn and I put in the electric and plumbing with Arch as our foreman. It was a good thing I knew something about this kind of work. I could not have done it without Elwyn, he did most of the hard work. The people of Flournoy and our church put the roof on our new house. People brought piles of clothes, some too big, some too small. There was one family, the Ampies, who brought an outfit for each child, the right size, all clean and nice and new. She told me they had a fire once and she got the same mess when their house burned down.

It was quite a job cleaning up the mess left from the fire. Arch took a couple loads of stuff to the dump. Evelyn and Clive stayed with us for a while. They left some of their things in our shop. They were burned also. We moved into our new home with no walls, just the framework and the roof. Thank goodness this was not a new experience for us. We moved into Rio Del Mar before it was finished. It did have walls though. Arch put up a four by six sheet of plywood on a couple of saw horses and that was our dinner table. I put a sheet on it for a tablecloth. The next morning I had to put a new sheet on the table because the chickens roosted on our dinner table. One time our horse Socks reached his head in the doorway and helped himself to a couple potatoes out of the hundred pound sack sitting just inside the door. He was a beautiful horse; chestnut brown and four white socks. Someone was always brushing him so he shined like a brand new penny. He was the favorite of the horses. Poor Monica and Lady seemed like plow horses next to him. Lady had a bad habit of trying to knock her rider off under the low branches. Monica would just plunk along, no real energy. But Socks was different. He would prance and buck and act like a racehorse when Arch was on him but he was gentle as a lamb for the younger children. Poor Socks met his demise by falling down the well behind our old house. It was horrible. We found him dead in the well. Elwyn had dumped everything from the fire down that well and covered it up. We never dreamed it was dangerous. I always believed that Socks saved at least one of my children's lives. If not him, one of my children could have been the one caught in that well. It was a very sad day. All the kids were crying as they all piled rocks on Socks.

One time I took care of Howard and Donna's children for a week when they went to Washington to visit her mom; Beth, Jeffery and little Kim. Kim was still taking a bottle when they left. I told her she did not need the bottle anymore and gave her a cup, she loved it. After that, no more bottle. Little Jeffery cried the whole first day, he missed his mom. Thank goodness June took over. Jeffery loved June. No more crying from Jeffery once mama June took over. June was seven. Beth loved Lorrie. She would get so excited when she saw Lorrie she would grab her by the head and bite her. Lorrie kept her distant for a while. Lorrie and Beth were eighteen months apart.

Harold had an auto accident and hurt his back. He couldn't work for three months. They moved in with us. We gave them our room. We took Eddie and Teddy's room and they were back on the sofas.

In 1961 we had to put Lorrie in the hospital. She had become dehydrated after a very bad cold. She had to stay in there for two whole weeks. It was very difficult for me. I knew then how my mother must have felt when I had to spend some time in the hospital when I was a child.

In 1962 I got quite a surprise. I thought for sure Lorrie was going to be my last baby but when Lorrie was five I found out we had another baby on the way. When I brought my new baby Elaine home from the hospital I gave her a nickname from the long line of trees just before our gate. Lane Tree fit her just right and I still call her that. Even though all my girls liked to play with dolls and dress-up in big girl clothes, Elaine seemed to be the most interested in playing with her dolls. She always wanted all the newest dolls that hit the market. Baby Alive was one in particular she had for the longest time. She really took care of that doll like it was a real baby. It even came with diapers because after you fed it, you would need to change its diapers. I wondered what they would think of next. I didn't have to wonder long. Elaine's next doll was only a head, one that you could set and style the hair in many different ways. She would curl, comb and style over and over. Maybe she got into the dolls so much because most of her brothers and sisters had already left or were leaving the nest and she had to find someone to play with.

In 1963 my dad died. I could not go to his funeral and this was hard for me. I was so glad we went back to see Mom, Dad and the rest of the family before

Elaine was born. Gene and Delores took care of Shirley and Lorrie. Diana, Arlene and June stayed with Nori and Donald. Eddie and Teddy we're with Evelyn

Diana, Laura and Shirley @ the Riverside Motel in Cloverdale, CA
1964

When we returned things got back to normal. Arlene and June used to run home from school and pick either the piano or the baby. Whoever got there first, got their choice.

Nori and Evelyn were both expecting. They both had boys. Evelyn's son Wayne was born in December and Nori's son Brett was born in March.

I now had ten children and four grandchildren and I was only thirty-seven years old. It really took courage to raise a family, which I did not realize I had. It was my family that gave me that courage. Sometimes I failed to live up to that. I always intended to follow through. I received quite a bit of benefits from my family. They all inspired me in my life, plus I learned a lot from them. I truly owe a lot to my children. They motivated me in more ways than I could mention. I thank God for my children. They taught me so much about life. They were always my first priority. I always prayed for guidance. I would never have made it without God's help.

The kid's seem to growing so fast. First Shirley graduated then Diana, soon Eddie and now Shirley was driving. We thought she was just too young to be driving so far. We lived almost twenty miles from town. The bus would pick them up for school but it was the after school things like the games and things that they wanted to drive to.

We decided to put the ranch up for sale. We sold it to a man called Robert Hoffsteader. He was actually famous. He and another German scientist won the Noble Peace Prize for splitting the atom in a fourth. He bought our place for a summer home. He had never shot a gun before. Arch showed him how to shoot. Boy did he love that. They were nice people. We were happy someone nice had our place

We bought a place in Red Bluff; four acres and a home with enough room for all the kids. Two of the acres had walnut and fruit trees. There was a nice big garden area that supplied us with an abundance of fresh vegetables. The kids enjoyed it very much. Sometimes when the field was flooded with irrigation Teddy would go out and get a fish. I think the water came from the Sacramento River. June and Arlene sold apricots from a little stand out in the front yard. We had intended on building a much larger one but we couldn't get the okay for that.

In 1964 we went looking for income property. It was either going to be Susanville or Cloverdale. We ended up buying The Riverside Motel just outside of Cloverdale. It had nine cabins and a three-bedroom home with an office. The first cabin was attached to the house so we ended up making Shirley, Diana, Arlene and June two bedrooms and a bath. It worked out fine. We put a door in the office to our part of the home.

In 1967 Eddie graduated from Cloverdale High School, Nori and Donald had a baby girl named Louise and Evelyn and Clive had a baby girl named Lela. Arch still worked as a carpenter and I ran the motel.

Life as a motel maid was much more work than I wanted so Arch and I thought it would be a better idea to make them monthly rentals. That worked out much better. Shirley, Diana and Eddie helped me paint the whole motel in one weekend.

Arch's sister Julia, her husband Jim and their daughter Jennie entered our lives again. They needed a place to stay. We had just bought a four-bedroom home on the other side of the river so we moved over there and Julia and Jim said they would take care of the monthly rentals. They moved into our place. Things did not work out so we moved back after six months. We rented them a cabin. Jennie was fifteen. She stayed with us quite often. In fact, it got to be such a habit she ended up moving in with us for a while. That didn't last for long. She moved back home and they all moved back to Cupertino.

After Shirley graduated from high school she worked at State Farm Insurance for a while. Then she lived with Gene and Delores for a while and went to College. In 1966 Shirley met Artie. My little girl is getting married. She made a dress for Elaine from her graduation dress so Elaine could be her flower girl. Elaine walked down the isle hanging on to Shirley's dress. Shirley and Art moved to Arizona. Art was in the Air Force.

Donald and Nori had a baby girl, Susan.

Diana ended up working for State Farm Insurance too. The funny thing was though, Shirley paid out some big money to an Employment Agency for the job she got there. Diana just answered an ad in the paper.

In 1967 Eddie worked in a restaurant as a cook. He was always buying Elaine something, he was very close to her. Eddie met a girl in the restaurant he worked in. her name was Karen. Eddie and Karen got married and had a daughter, Keri.

In 1968 Diana and Elaine and I went to Arizona to be with Shirley when she was going to have her first baby. Little Christine was born. On the way there we experienced our first flash flood. The car spun out of control. When we finally came to a stop Elaine was so mad at me she wouldn't talk to either of us for the rest of the way there. I guess she thought I did it on purpose or something. She sure was angry.

We bought forty acres west of Healsburg from a man we worked for occasionally, Mr. Reynolds. The property was advertised in Sunset Magazine back in 1934. The property was thick with beautiful, giant redwood trees. There were a couple of cabins on the place that had Russian designs on the exterior and interior. We were told it once belonged to a Russian Ambassador. What a haven. We had to cross the creek five or six times just to get back there. It kind of made you feel like you were in a different place in another time. There was wildlife all over; deer and wild boar. Two springs provided fresh water year round. The first time we went to go look at the property Arch and I went for a long walk. We climbed way up this mountain so we could see as much as we could of the property. We were almost to the top when I lost my footing and down I went, rolling and bouncing down the mountainside like a sack of potatoes. I saw trees and big rocks out of the corner of my eye as I went whizzing past. I can't believe I didn't hit one of them. After about a thirty foot decent I came to stop with a thud right on my face. Arch thought I was surely dead. I sat up and yelled to him that I was all right. I felt little pieces of something in my mouth that I thought for sure were my teeth but it turned out to be the piece of gum I was chewing. Arch helped me up and we walked back to the cabin where Donald and Gene were. Arch took me to the doctor. The doctor gave me a shot of something and told me to go home and go to bed. I still felt fine. Looking back I'm sure I was in shock. When we got home Shirley took one look at me and fainted. Arch wanted her to help him take me to bed. Shirley fainted again. I must have looked a mess. I ended up staying in bed for a week. The first three days I don't even remember. I was hurt more than I knew.

Gene bought one of the forty acre parcels and really put a lot of effort into making this a place we all enjoyed visiting.

Between 1964 and 1967 so much went on. A man we knew wanted to buy our motel. He had a three-bedroom home on forty acres, half in alfalfa, in Vale, Oregon. He also had a two-bedroom home in Salt Lake City Utah. He was willing to trade us both his properties plus twenty thousand dollars for our motel. Arch took the deal sight on seen.

Nori, Donald, Brett and Louise lived in Yreka. We packed up and went to Yreka to see them on the way to Oregon. It was hard for me to leave. I just left three children, which I was not ready for. Things were moving too fast. When we got to Nori and Donald's they told us about a house for sale; a big two-story place for sale cheap. I sure liked it. It wasn't too far away from their house. We signed a six-month lease to see if we wanted it. This was January. Yreka was cold; snow and ice. Arlene and June were in high school. Teddy, Lorrie and Lane Tree were in grade school. Arch did not like it there because there was just not enough work for him. When the six-month lease was up, we packed up and went to Oregon. It was hard for Arlene and June to go to another school again. The younger ones didn't mind it so much.

When we got to Vale, Oregon we stopped and got a hamburger. I think it was the biggest hamburger I ever saw. We looked the town over a bit and headed out to see our new home for the first time. The house seemed to be sitting out all alone on this huge piece of property. There weren't many trees, not like Flournoy or Healsburg, so it seemed kind of desolated. Oh there were a few houses scattered here and there but not many.

Life in Vale was not happy for me. June and Arlene adjusted to their new school but the rules were different in here. In California the girls wore their skirts quite a bit shorter than this school allowed to I was called in to the office in short order. I should have been a little more selective in what I wore that day but I didn't think anything of it until I caught sight of myself in the school windows as I was going in. I had on a bright orange, two-piece skirt and jacket. The skirt was a little tight and kind of short. I felt like Harper Valley PTA. The song was popular then. Well, I settled the issue with the principal and we agreed to let down our hems a little.

We were looking for a church to attend. Our neighbor went to a Nazarene Church. There were many different churches in town and everyone wanted us to go to theirs. We never did settle on one. We just went to all of them. Arlene got a job helping out a family down the road. A man and his two sons were in need of a little domestic help since his wife was disabled. Turns out he was looking for more that just a maid. Arlene moved back home.

Arch rented a huge store and took items on consignment. He hired an auctioneer and we had auctions on Friday and Saturday nights. The girls ran the snack stand and Teddy helped his dad. I took care of the books. Elaine was by my side with her little pen and paper. She really thought she was helping. We had twenty acres of alfalfa to irrigate and take care of. We were busy all the time.

Just like all the other business ventures Arch ever got into, he soon grew tired of it. We sold the store. We went back to California to visit Lela and Harold. I did not want to go back to Vale. We sold our place in Salt Lake City.

I was always looking for a business we could do together. It was getting harder and harder for Arch to work. His ulcers bothered him all the time. I read an ad in the paper about a restaurant for sale in Cottonwood. There was a small house in the back. I really wanted this place. It was perfect. I could be close to my relatives and put my children to work with me. This was the first time I realized that I all I really had to do was speak up a little and I could have a say in were we lived. We bought the restaurant. It was a small place, holding twenty people max. It was summer. I was glad to be back in warm California and running a business that I really knew how to do, cook. Diana came home to live for a while. The relationship she had going just didn't work out and I was glad she came home. Besides, little Amy was on the way. Diana, Arlene and June were the waitresses. Lorrie poured coffee and Arch and Ted kept things clean and organized. Arch said we should call the place Laura's Kitchen and so we did. As it turns it we did very well there. Before we started we went back to Vale to get our things. We put most of our stuff in storage and moved in the tiny place behind the restaurant. The house didn't even have a kitchen but it sure was okay with the kids. They got to eat in the restaurant three meals a day. We lived there for three months then bought a place about a mile away. This restaurant we bought was never so busy before. Arlene and June were cute little waitresses and we were packed all the time. The younger crowd came for the girls and the older, and younger ones, came for the food. One day I notice just how short those girls' skirts were when they were bending over to scoop the ice cream from the freezer. The next day the girl's uniforms turned to pants. I loved working at Laura's Kitchen. Most of my family was right there with me. The only ones that were not involved were Gene, Donald, Shirley and Ed. Ed came a lot though. It made me feel good to know I could serve a good meal that everyone would enjoy. There was a lot of hard work for everyone but fun times also. Ed ended up having an operation on his throat. That was the reason he always had a huge glass of water when he ate. He had a growth in his throat. Everything turned out all right. I was sad that he suffered for so many years with that problem and it was never discovered. Arch played a big part in the success of the restaurant. He was a very good public relations man. He always wore a white chef's hat, a white shirt and a bow tie. He talked to the customer's and made them feel at home. He made sure everyone was enjoying their meal. He also taught the girls how to treat everyone.

Laura, Art, Ted and friend @ Laura's Kitchen, Cottonwood, CA
1968

I know God played the biggest part in our success. We would never have gotten anywhere without his guidance. I always felt that whatever talent I had, God gave it to me. It was up to me to take it from there and use it the best way I could. Sometimes that is not an easy task. We have a ruler and a judge; someone is watching over all of us and loves us unconditionally. No matter what you do, you always get a chance to do better if you listen. Not just one chance either, quite a few chances. All you have to do to earn this is to love him and obey his laws. Some laws are not easy to obey but they are for our own good whether we know it at the time or not. I love how he speaks to us as a parent would at Psalms 32:8 "I shall make you have insight and instruct you in the way you should go. I will give advice with my eye upon you."

Nori and Donald were living close by too. They were running a pie shop. We bought pies from them sometimes. The restaurant got so busy sometimes there was standing room only. Lela came and worked for us part time. Shirley had her second little girl, Sharon. Shirley and Art moved from Arizona to Chicago. Arts parents lived there. My children were having babies instead of me, about time.

We traded our place in Vale to a man in Cottonwood that had forty acres in Whitmore. Turns out he knew Vale very well. I had entered a contest and won a pony complete with saddle and all. He had a great home up on the Whitmore property. There was already one horse on the property so he had some company. We went up on Sundays and rode them.

We sold the Whitmore property and made a handsome profit. Another adventure was soon on its way. A new housing development was going up in Cottonwood. They called the project River Lakes Ranch. The company flew people out to look at the property and entertained them for the weekend. They were looking for some caterers and we took the job. We ended up preparing a barbeque meal for anywhere from fifty to hundred people each weekend. We fixed barbeque beef, chicken and ham, homemade potato salad, ranch-style beans and homemade applesauce; we actually peeled all the apples ourselves. They had square dances on Saturday night so the customers were well fed and entertained. It certainly helped sales. One big perk we got was all the green stamps from the groceries. S&H green stamps that is. You would paste them in a book and redeem them for household items like toasters and mixers and coffee pots. We were so busy we ended up selling the restaurant. In 1970 Arlene married Bob and they moved to San Diego. Bob was in the Navy. She ended up staying in San Diego for three months before Bob went to sea. Then Arlene moved home and helped us with the catering business. Diana, June and Arlene were so much help for us, we were so busy. Unfortunately this only lasted for about a year and a half. There was a plane crash, which killed the manager of the outfit that was running the project. They instantly stopped bringing people in and the whole thing just fizzled out for some time. It was strange not working. I didn't know what to do with myself. No problem. Something always happens to keep me busy or entertained.

Diana went into labor. It wasn't long before little Amy was born. Amy lit up all of our lives. June and Arlene and I loved her like she was our own. She was so cute and petite.

Arch was very close to her too. Poor Arch was not doing well. He had to go into the hospital and have a kidney removed. I was glad so many of the kids were home at that time. It felt like old times again. Diana and little Amy, Arlene, June, Teddy, Lorrie and Lane Tree made for a full house but a happy one. Diana and Amy soon needed a place of their own and moved to Redding. Boy did we miss that baby, and Diana too of course. Diana went to work as a waitress at the Green Barn in Redding. There was a nice looking man named Bill who bartended there and they soon became an item.

In 1972 Arlene gave birth to a daughter, Cheri. She had her at the Balboa Navel Hospital in San Diego. I was disappointed I couldn't be there with her but

Arch was so sick I just couldn't leave. When Cheri was three months old Bob went overseas again and Arlene came back home to live for a while.

Diana and Bill were married in 1973. Bill had six children. Diana became a new bride and a mother of seven for Diana. What a wonderful mother she was.

Ed was now divorced from his first wife Kris and the manager of a Denny's restaurant. When Denny's sold the place it became the Lime Tree. June and her friend Kathy went to work there. June fell head over heels for the handsome cook that worked there. His name was Steve. Ed became involved with Kathy's sister Annette. Before you know it they were both married and starting a new life. They also had a couple of friends Rod and Cindy that worked there. That was a fun place for them. They all got along and worked well together. They were all familiar with restaurant work and did well.

Shirley had another baby, a boy this time; Michael. Now I had nineteen grandchildren.

My mom died. It had been four years since I'd seen her. We wrote each other once a week. I missed her letters. My mom was quite a lady. She did the best she knew how with all her children. At 4' 11" we all towered over her but she was boss. In her last letter to me she told me to always keep in contact with my brothers and sisters and I have. I will miss my mom. I know now all the many things she had to go through with a house full of children. I always thought my mom was sort of a primadonna that really didn't do much around the house. Wonder why when I think of her I remember how she used to put on that apron every morning. Funny how you realize the reality of many things when you get older.

Teddy said he didn't want to be called Teddy anymore so we started calling him Ted.

I went back to work as a cook at a smorgasboard called North's Chuck Wagon. Of all the places I ever worked this one was by far the most taxing. I worked so hard here. Sometimes it was almost comical. The giant pots and pans in that kitchen were almost bigger than me. There were fifteen-inch frying pans and twenty-gallon pots. The roasts and hams were the biggest I had ever seen in my whole life and I never stop frying chicken. I was swimming in side dishes of potatoes, veggies and rice. I made cinnamon rolls, bread pudding and a number of other desserts. There was one person who just made all the salads. The person that had the title of night cook, never really cooked, they just served what I prepared and cleaned everything up. I started at six and worked until three. Most of the time I worked there I never knew what a break was and usually started early and left late. I was exhausted most of the time. Lorrie was still living at home at that time and I was so thankful for her domestic help. She kept the house neat and tidy. I paid her fifteen dollars a week. Ted was a bit rebellious. It was hard for him. Dad never really gave him the quality time that a dad should, being so sick and all. I was always either working or tired. Teenagers can get restless without the proper attention from their parents. I had to work though, Arch was just too sick.

Arch had another operation. This time they took out half of his stomach. He had been through quite a bit with his bad health but he always kept going. I truly do not know how he survived as long as he did.

In 1974 Lorrie married her boyfriend Daren. He was in the Army. Arlene and Bob got a divorce. Bob re-married and Arlene had a boyfriend named Frank and Arlene never did get married but they stayed together for about six or seven years until she got tired of his abuse of drugs and left.

After a long battle with cancer Harold died leaving my sister Lela all alone. Arch and I would go over every Friday night for the next six months just to comfort her. I had to hand it to Lela though. All those years with Harold, Lela never did drive. At sixty-two she went out and learned how to drive and got her license. I was very proud of her for that. Lorrie and Daren only lasted for a few years. She had two girls with him, Shannon and Natasha. When Lorrie found out that Daren was unfaithful to her she called and asked me what to do. I told her to do whatever she thought she needed to do and I would support her decision even if it meant divorce. I actually wanted to encourage her to leave. I did not want her to go through what I did. She was living in Oregon at the time so Arch and I went up and got her and the kids and brought them home with us for a while.

We stopped and visited Gene and Delores who were living in Lake Oswego, Oregon. It was nice to see Joanne, Linda and Jimmy too.

Lorrie ended up moving in with June and Steve for a while. June and Steve did not have any children at that time so June was loving every minute of those babies of Lorrie's. She and Steve both loved them as their own.

Arch was enjoying some better health and embarked on another adventure by buying an ice cream truck. He did rather well too. Some of the kids took a route or two and it was a fun adventure, and plenty of ice cream for all.

Ted moved to San Jose. He went to work at Winchells Donuts as a baker. He met and married a girl named Cindy. They named their first boy Scotty. Shirley also had another child, a girl named Denise. In 1975 Ted and Cindy had their second child, a girl, Tonya. Ted and Cindy moved to Portland.

That same year Arch was diagnosed with lung cancer. Arch was a heavy smoker. To tell you the truth, as much as he smoked, I can't believe I was never affected by second-hand smoke. He smoked in the car, in the house, everywhere.

I am so glad I never took up that horrible habit. Arch refused to have another operation though.

Shirley ended up moving back to California with her four children and leaving her husband. I was never glad that any of my daughters divorced but some things you just can't forgive or forget.

We sold our house in Cottonwood and moved to Redding, closer to my work. Elaine was the only child left at home now. Art sold the ice cream truck and bought a hot dog truck. He called it the Wheelie Weenie. Diana's husband Bill helped him put in the steam tables and a refrigerator. Steve painted it and made all the signs. It looked great. Arch always had to have something to do.

Lorrie re-married in 1979 to a man named Tom. The next year they had a baby girl, Leah.

Then in 1982 they had a little boy and named him Sean. In 1983 Lorrie and Tom divorced. I had a bad auto accident in the spring of 1984. Someone hit me from the side and spun me around right in the middle of the road. The police urged me to go to the hospital and get checked out, I refused because I thought I was just a little shaken but fine. I actually went to work. June was working at North's Chuck Wagon too, as a waitress. When she showed up at work and she saw my car it scared the heck out of her. She was so happy to see I was alright. I looked alright on the outside anyway but there was trouble inside brewing. My boss came in and saw me and made one of the girls take me to the hospital. I ended up being off work for three months. I tried to go back to work after that but I couldn't do it. I had to quit. My back was really giving me problems. We needed some kind of income so Arch and I became the caretakers of a mini storage place. I remember one incident at the mini storage place that Elaine will never forget. She begged her dad to drive his truck around the storage buildings. Well, she was a very inexperienced driver and ended up plowing into one of the storage units and totaling her dad's truck. Since keeping the books for the storage place was not really a full-time job, I started cooking for the forestry. I worked four days and nights and Lela worked the same. This only lasted about a year. Arch did not want me to be away from him that much. I did love that job though.

Don and Nori divorced and Nori moved to Redding. She and I ended up opening a pie shop. The pie shop was fun but a short-lived adventure. The city was putting in a new road and we could not have walk in traffic to the shop.

Elaine moved in with her boyfriend Ron. I was not happy about that but then I what could I do. Arch and I were now all alone. It seemed very strange. Diana and Bill invited us to stay out at their place in Red Bluff until we figured out what we wanted to do. I got a job as the Welcome Wagon Lady. It was another fun but short-lived adventure. I did meet some nice people. I was offered a job at the Alcoholic Recovery Center. They needed someone who could plan, shop for and prepare three meals a day for the twenty residents there. I took the job. It was easy enough for me. I had been cooking for at least that many people all my life. We moved into town in a little apartment just down the road from where I worked. It was great. Arch could even come to work and hang out with me whenever he wanted. I was glad to have him close, his health was failing very rapidly.

CHAPTER 12

▼

Arch was needed more and more care. Gene sent us one thousand dollars so I could take a leave of absence from work and tend to Arch. Lela helped me sometimes. Arch was failing fast. Hospice came to my rescue near the end of his battle with cancer. I was worn to a frazzle. Arch died on October 28, 1981.

It was hard to watch someone you love so much die a slow, painful death. There is absolutely nothing you can do but pray for strength to get through it. People told me it was a good thing that Arch died since he had been suffering for so long. I was glad he was no longer suffering but the suffering just began for me. They never knew the loss. Arch and I were together for thirty-three years. We had good times and bad but mostly good. I really never showed my pain to many people. I would put up a good front but when I was alone, behind my closed doors or in my bed at night, I would cry my eyes out. I would miss him very much.

I went to Gene and Delores' for a month. It was good for me. There were plenty of grandchildren around and this helped me a lot.

Delores, Linda and Joanne had a knit shop. Linda could make anything. It was a busy place. I sure enjoyed the time I spent with them. We went there everyday.

It was nice visiting but it was also nice to get home. I had some wonderful friends in Red Bluff; Claudine, Donna, Geneva, Kitty, Paula, Karen and Kathie. Most of them worked as waitress at the Green Barn. Donna had a way of keeping everyone going. If I didn't show up for our weekly lunch she would call me up and tell me to get my butt over there. She always kept me up.

In December of 1981 I had a hysterectomy. Nori had one the month before. We all spent Christmas at Nori's house. It sure was strange without Art and

Donald there. My kids were all on their own now too so it was quite a different life for me.

I started night classes with Geneva at a Shasta College course offered in Red Bluff. I would study on my breaks at work. You're never too old to learn something new. I was fifty-seven. I thought I was old then. I took psychology, nutrition and a police community class. One evening a week I made china dolls. I made a doll for each of my children. Each month I would put out on display whatever doll of the kid who was having a birthday. It helped remind me of their little days. As far as I'm concerned though, they will always be little to me.

My nights and days were full. Working at the recovery center and going to school kept my mind busy and I didn't have time to think about being lonely. But when it was evening and I was at home, I was unhappy. I think I was keeping so busy because I just did not want to have to deal with all the confusion going on in my head.

In 1983 I quit my job at the recovery center. I really don't know why, I liked the job. I think I needed to get out of my apartment where Arch died. There were too many sad memories and it was time to move on.

I moved to Redding, got an apartment and a new job. I started working as a counselor for teenage runaways. My group consisted of nineteen, ill-mannered girls. Boy what a handful they were. Another lady named Roxanne and I managed this group. On the weekends I worked at the Wilcox Golf Course. I assisted the head cook. It was fun working there. That counseling job didn't last long, too much trouble.

I moved in with Lela. I wanted to help her but she did not want me to go to work. I could not sit and watch television all day. I felt very sorry for Lela. I had so much energy and she had none. It was not her fault, she had a bad heart. I wanted to help her but I wasn't doing her any good staying there. I was working at the golf course. The people at the counseling place called and asked if I would come back to work. I said I would if I only had to deal with no more than six girls. They agreed and I went back. It was a lot easier because the girls I was helping now were really trying to get out on their own and just needed some guidance on issues like, how to find a job, how to dress for it, how to buy a car, or even how to take care of a child. I taught them the importance of having confidence in themselves and self-respect. I felt good because most of the girls took to heart the things I taught them and they advanced. I ended up being a good friend to most of them.

In 1984 Arlene married a man she had been with for a few years. His name was Wally. He was a nice enough guy that is when he wasn't drinking. He had a real problem with alcohol but Arlene stuck with him and kept hoping he would change. During one of his "dry spells" things were going pretty good for them. They found a house in Redding that was big enough for them and Cheri and had a kind of mother-in-law quarters. We all moved in that house together. It was fun for a while but trouble was brewing. Wally just could not stay away from the alcohol and it caused so many problems for Arlene they finally split up and we all moved out of the house and went our separate ways.

This is when I became a clown. Lolly the Clown was born and I really felt I had found my nitch. I opened up a shop with Shirley. She made the appointments and designed the costumes. I was doing children's parties. What fun I had and I got paid for it too. I charged seven dollars and fifty cents per child with a ten child minimum. I bought party favors, hats and prizes for each child. Shirley also made puppets for a puppet show and a Lolly doll for the birthday child. Between the puppet show, the games and singing songs it would take about an hour for a party. Sometimes I would go straight from one party to another. I did enjoy it though when I had time to go home and take a little break between shows. Shirley was so talented. She even made me a Santa suit. At Christmas I could be Santa or Lolly whichever gig I wanted. Quite a combo.

Elaine married Larry and in 1986 their son Andrew was born. That day really stands out in my mind because that same day the shuttle exploded killing seven people aboard.

It really distressed me but there will always be stress in your life you have to deal with. If you remember that God will help you with any load you have to bear you'll get through.

Lorrie married Mike. He had two children already, Holly and T.J. With Lorrie's four they had a houseful. In 1988 June and Steve became the proud parents of a sweet little girl named Cyera. Elaine and Larry had a sweet little girl too, Nicole.

In 1989 Ed married Doris. She had two boys, Bill and Josh. Arlene married Mel. He had two girls Tiffany and Alaina. Add nine more grandchildren to my list.

My dear sister Lela died of an enlarged heart. I miss her.

So many deaths and births it was hard to keep up. Loved ones dieing, loved ones being born, children marrying. I enjoyed my grandchildren very much. We had so much fun when we were all together in all the parades. My first little clowns were Cheri, Shannon, Tasha, Denise and Michael. They followed my lead. They were so cute that they won the judges hearts and votes most of the time. We acquired many trophies. The next group of little clowns were Leah,

Sean, Cyera and little Andrew who was only three. One afternoon we were all at his house getting ready for the parade when he told me he wanted to be a clown too. So Shirley, whiz that she was, made him up a clown suit as quick as you please. He was adorable. The other kids pulled him in a wagon. We won second prize. Sean didn't like the idea that we won second prize. He was so used to us winning first or even grand prize that he just didn't want to settle for any less. We were in a store after the parade and we all had our ribbons on, all of us except Sean that is. A man noticed that Sean did not have his ribbon on like the rest of us and must have overheard some of our conversation about Sean being so disgruntled. He took the liberty of telling Sean he should be happy he won second prize because he had been in parades for years and never won anything at all. After hearing that Sean wanted to wear his ribbon and he was proud of it too. I have so many wonderful memories with my grandchildren as clowns as well as just coming over to spend the night and watch a movie or paint a picture, or work in the yard. My grandchildren and great-grandchildren still fill my life to the brim.

The people that bought the hot dog truck, The Wheelie Weenie, did not do well with it and I got it back. I moved in a little home in Central Valley and the main road was in front of my house. I was now a hot dog maker. I had fun for a while. Some of my grandchildren helped me. Sharon, Cheri, Denise, Michael, Shannon, Amy, Sean and Leah would come over and help me run the truck and spend the night. Sometimes one or two, and a few times all of them came at once. What fun we had. June and Steve took the Wheelie Weenie up to Shingletown and it became a part of their yogurt shop. They did a fantastic business in the summer but because business fell off so much in the winter they were forced to close.

Donald had a home in Cottonwood. I rented it for a while then moved to Redding.

In 1989 tragedy struck for Donald, Nori and their daughter Susan. Susan's little boy Todd drowned in a swimming pool. It was the worst thing that happened in our whole family. The entire family was devastated. It is difficult to get through a death but almost impossible when it is a child.

In 1990 June and Steve became the proud parents of a little boy named Skylar.

This same year I fell and hurt my back pretty bad and I gave up being a clown. A few of the last parties I booked there were times when I would try to get up from the floor and would topple right over. The kids laughed their heads off, they thought it was part of the act.

Laura as "Lolly The Clown" with my littlest clown at the time
Nicole Toothman (Elaine's daughter)
1989

CHAPTER 13

▼

In 1991 I began yet another chapter in my life. One thing I can say, my life was never dull. I was sixty-two and I could not get my social security, some mix-up in the system so they said. I took Arch's social security, which amounted to a whole one hundred and forty dollars a month. So I went out and found a job. I went to work helping the elderly. I found plenty of work. I wasn't going to be able to collect mine until I was sixty-nine so I had to find something to do. I remembered my dad talking about social security when I was thirteen. I don't know how I got old so fast.

Warren had an eye removed, it was cancerous. That never put a damper on his sense of humor though. I always enjoyed our telephone conversations. Mary and I would call each other pretty regular too.

My little Eddie was in a logging accident and lost his leg. He suffered though so much pain for a few years with trying to save it. Finally he made which turned out to be the best decision to have it removed. He progressed rapidly and it probably saved his life. His wife Doris has always been very supportive.

All my daughter-in-laws and son-in-laws have always been just like my own. I am so happy it turned out that way. Actually, I consider myself extremely fortunate it did. I am truly blessed to have such a beautiful family. Each time a new person entered my life it was as if my bowl of cherries would overflow.

I was always on the move. I had so many short-term jobs. Most of them I enjoyed but never really found the right nitch like when I was a clown. I was working in a nursing home five days a week as a cook. I enjoyed that job. There were only six ladies in the home. I liked having a small group. It gave me more freedom to fix them dishes they really liked. I sang old songs while I cooked and some of them would pass by the kitchen, sometimes stopping and joining in. On the weekends I ran a doughnut shop. I worked for ten percent of the sales. I hired two of my granddaughters, Susan and Sharon as waitresses. I was always involved with my grandchildren somehow.

Warren came to visit. Shirley, Warren and I went on a train trip where we were involved in a murder mystery. Warren was a judge, Shirley was a librarian and I was a busybody columnist. It was so much fun. A long-time Shasta County Judge Eaton was on the trip too and played himself. Shirley made our dresses.

I went to work for my friend Virginia's sister, Dee. I was her caregiver. Virginia and I became very good friends. Dee hated being old and she took it out on every on around her. She was a handful. Virginia was happy someone else was taking care of Dee. There was never any pleasing Dee. I worked longer for Dee only because of Virginia. Otherwise I would have quite that job much sooner.

Virginia and I would go to the Moose Lodge and swim or exercise then have a glass of wine by the pool before I went to work at Dee's. I would be careful not to come in with wet hair otherwise she would give me a bad time about having fun at the Moose with Virginia. I invited Dee to go with us but she never wanted to. She just wanted to complain. I truly tried to make her happy but nothing worked. She was bitter and stayed bitter until the day she died. What a waste. After Dee died I quit working for the elderly.

My sister Betty died of a brain tumor. She had been suffering for a long time. I was so glad I made the trip back to see her a few years before. For someone in so much pain Betty still looked beautiful. I was glad I got to see my little brother Bobby, Kathie,

Rick, her children, Mary's family Dolly, Johnny, Charlie, Teddy's daughter Kathie and her children. It was also wonderful seeing my little brother Bobby, his wife Margie, Warren and his three daughters, Joelen, Shelly, and Liza. Warren bought me three plane tickets and took me to Branson, Missouri to so many shows I lost count.

Warren had always been such a good brother to me.

June and Steve added another baby boy to their family, little Michael.

Charlie's wife Helen died. I'm so glad Charlie's three children were around to help him. I got on a kick of making bread for a while, two loaves a week. Shirley would stop by and get her loaf. Shirley and I did a lot of things together. She really helped me through some lonely years and many trying times.

In 1998 Diana's husband Bill died of cancer. They had been married for twenty-five years. We had so many good times out at their place. With Amy gone and married to Trevor, Diana was all alone. She sold the ranch and moved into town. She loved working in the yard and it showed; looked like something out of Better Homes and Gardens. She always did love working in the yard, even as a kid.

Virginia and I started making small items like children's chairs, benches and tables. We painted and decorated all kinds of things and took them to the craft fairs. I loved it when Virginia used to call me with one of her new ideas and we would put our heads together and pound some nails. Lorrie's husband Mike provided much of the lumber we used in our projects. Boy what fun these two old ladies had sawing, pounding, painting flowers, Indian Art, cartoons and anything else we could think of. We made a few mistakes but that just gave us something to laugh about. Matter of fact, we laugh quite a bit. Every time we messed up on some project we would just say, "We can hide it with paint." I wasn't quite as particular about things as Virginia; she wanted everything perfect. We poked fun at each other, always kidding around. Virginia's husband Fletcher was happy to see her enjoying herself. Sometimes Fletcher would help us out by doing the sanding on some projects. Virginia and Fletcher lived up on a hill in Old Shasta. Virginia also had a small cabin next to her daughter and son-in-law's house, Ethellen and Don. We would go over there to paint. Sometimes Ethellen would make a barbeque at the cabin for a few family members. They had three daughters; Ethellen, Heather and Carline. Her granddaughter Jennifer was always close by. We always had fun no matter what we were doing. We even tried to make frames for the pictures we painted. One time Don said he wanted to have an auction at his place and we could bring all our painting and he would auction them off. Our families came and bought everything we had. It was so much fun. I felt like Gramma Moses.

I remember one time Virginia and I went to a lumber company and climbed in their dumpster for pieces of wood to use for our projects. Talk about a limited budget. We sure got a kick out this. We must have looked a sight; two old ladies dumpster diving.

There are no words for the satisfaction we got from our efforts. We always made enough money for our trips. Virginia had a small motor home. We used to pile our wood crafts into it and off we would go to whatever craft fair that was within a hundred mile distance. What ever we didn't sell we would save for the next one or give to our grandkids. It didn't matter how much we made because most of it was just having fun. We were two Grannies on the go. I never had a friend like Virginia before. We both liked the same things and enjoyed the fact that we were able to go and do what ever we wanted, whenever we wanted. We were free birds having a blast.

Sometimes we would go to wineries and sit outside, eat our lunch and taste the wine. What a life. I think we had just as much fun in the parking lots watching the busloads of people go in and out. I will always cherish my fun times with Virginia.

Ted moved to Portland and got a job with Wheaton Trucking. When he passed through Redding he would stop and take me to dinner or I would fix him dinner. I am very proud of him. He had been through quite a bit but he came through with flying colors. I wish I could have been there more for him when he was a teenager. I was just working too much.

In 1992 Don moved to Idaho. Shirley, Virginia and I went to visit. We showed up at his place with breakfast, anything we didn't have to cook; bagels, cream cheese and strawberry jam. We had fun at Donald's. Donald called Virginia Ms. Marmalade because one time we were making marmalade and it burned. Don blamed it on Virginia but she didn't care. The name stuck, just like the jam on the bottom of the pan.

On one trip we went to Shoshoni. Virginia's brother Jim and his wife Lorraine lived there. The whole town was involved in the craft show. We set up everything we made and I wore my clown suit and did a little entertaining. We sold everything we had at that show. We arrived with a full motor home and left empty. Virginia's son Don was with us. We rented a cabin that had hot springs. We put on our swimsuits and stepped in. What a relaxing time. I hung a few paintings around to make it feel like home. Don was staying at Jim's, one thing he never lets me forget.

I made a fish ball to eat on the way. Virginia made split pea soup. What a combination. Don't knock it until you try it; it was good.

On one trip we went to Gene & Delores' cabin in Healsburg. I couldn't believe Virginia's motor home made it over all the creeks. We only got stuck one time but we got out. We messed up one bumper but that didn't stop us. We kept going with the bumper sticking straight out. Their whole family was there; Joanne, Dave, Jon, Linda, Delores, Kristen, Allie, Mallory, Jimmy and Dona. Gene and Linda did all the cooking. What fun we had. We went to one of the creeks. I was acting silly so I put sand all over my legs. My little grandchildren did the same. I truly love being a kid and that clown in me loves to come out from time to time.

From there we went to meet Virginia's family at Orick on the coast. The ocean was beautiful and at Orick you could park your motor home free right near the beach. One time we decided to put up a big tent. We tried anyway. If you can picture Lucy and Ethel wrapped up in a tent that would be me and Virginia. We finally got the tent up and our pads down for our beds. Wow, those pads were a long way down and a longer way getting back up the next morning. Virginia was crawling all around the tent trying to find something. I was wrapped up in the side of the tent and could get out. We were laughing and yelling at the same time. Don came running over to help us thinking maybe a raccoon or something had gotten into our tent. We all got a big laugh out of it but no more tents after that. We Motel-ed it after that. Besides, they ended up taking away our free parking for motor homes. No matter where you stayed though, the ocean was always beautiful.

On one of our adventures we rented a houseboat on Shasta Lake. There were ten of us, Virginia and I, Don and Ethellen and a few of their friends. We went out for seven days. Each day two people picked a country. For our day, Virginia and I choose Mexico. We only had to cook one day, breakfast, lunch and dinner. We also supplied beverages and an evening snack. We made Margaritas with gummy worms. Everyone was served like royalty. What fun we had. I wore a pair of tap shoes and tapped everywhere I went. All they had to do was snap their fingers and we were there. Then off to Jamaica, then Monte Carlo and Morocco and New Orleans. Last stop was Texas. Everyone had their own napkins, tablecloth and flag of where we were going. One of the couples had a small boat they tied up along side the houseboat. It was great. For six days Virginia and I were wined and dined and didn't have to do a thing. I truly don't know which was more fun, serving or being served. I would love to do that again. When we got back to the dock we all pitched in and cleaned the boat up ship shape. It was a great bunch. I am so glad I went.

In 1994 my dear friends Donna, Geneva and Kitty wanted me to meet their friend Bill. I went to church with him a few times and dinner. He was such a nice person. Three months after we met his doctor said he had cancer. They sent him to U.C. Davis. He was there forty-four days. I stayed in Sacramento in a McDonald's house and saw him every day. When he came home I still went to church with him and came over and fixed him something to eat. He was not eating very good.

In 1995 Donna, Howard's wife died. She was only fifty. Her pace maker stopped. I sure missed her. She was one of my best buddies. Bill's brother and sister were coming out for a visit. Bill asked me to marry him. This was quite upsetting for both of us. We both knew he was not going to live very long but I granted him his wish. I did care for him a great deal. He was a very kind man. When Bill's family arrived we got married. Bill died three weeks later. I kind of went into a tailspin. I lost two people I cared very much about. I wasn't working on any projects or painting or anything. I still visited my family and went to the Moose with Virginia but I was kind of in a fog.

I have so many grandchildren and great grandchildren by now it is hard to keep track of them all. But what a joy for me to have so many people in my life that I care about and that care about me. My daughters' husbands are my sons and my son's wives are my daughters. Many of my children have stepchildren but I don't have any step-grandchildren. They all call be Gramma and I wouldn't have it any other way.

Glen Dork
and
Laura Vanbibber-Roza-Feise- Dork
2000

Gene

Don & Ted

Ed, June, Shirley, Lorrie,
Laura, Arlene,
Elaine, Diana

Nora & Glenda Dork

CHAPTER 14

▼

Well, here it is 1997 and we have come full circle. This was the year I became a Dork and decided it was time to write down some of the things that happened to me during my life. What was my answer to Glen's proposal?

Glen and I were married. When my son Ted came back from Mexico he was very surprised. I was a little surprised myself. I guess Glen was right when he said I belonged to him way back when we first met at the Poker Run. Glen was seventy-one but we felt just like a couple of kids. It's no fun growing old if you can't act like a kid sometimes. I like being childish. It makes me feel good. You don't stop laughing because you're growing old, you grow old if you stop laughing. Have fun, laugh your head off, act like a kid if you want to. Life is too short. I have had a lot of laughter in my life and I am not going to stop now. I got a good laugh at the look on his face when I told him I had ten children. He actually took it rather well. Especially when I told him that he was now not only Dad to his two and my ten, he was also Grandpa to about fifty or so more.

I have always been one to give the people close to me nicknames. Glen got Little Jimmy Dickens or Baby Boy. He enjoyed the attention. I really enjoyed the fact that Glen was a spiritual man. He read the Bible every day, sang in the choir and attended Bible classes and church on Sunday. He was a good man but he could be a real bear sometimes.

Glen had a beloved friend named Stace who was a vicar in his church. He was just like a son to him. As our marriage grew Stace was a big part of Glen's and my life. He helped me bring out the gentle and kind man inside of Glen. Stace was Glen's best man at our wedding. My daughter Shirley was my maid of honor. Here we had dozens of people to choose from that lived locally and we choose the two people that lived out of state. Shirley came out from Texas and Stace came all the way out from Louisiana. Now I was officially a Dork. Stace is now a pastor at our Trinity Lutheran Church.

We started traveling right away and enjoyed it very much. We visited his family, then we visited my family. Then we visited people we didn't even know.

We were having so much fun we put a sticker on the back of our van. We called ourselves "The Traveling Dorks". We even got business cards made up that read the same. We sure had a lot of fun with it. We gave away a lot of cards too. People wanted them as souvenirs.

In 2000 Glen sold his place and I sold mine. Glen gave Nora and Glenda the little house that Nora was, and still is, living in. With what we both profited from the sales of our homes we bought a little place in town. We both sold our vans and bought one van that we used to start traveling. We became the Traveling Dorks. We went to visit my sisters and brothers in Nebraska. Teddy and Mary weren't doing well. I'm glad Glen got to meet them. Charlie, Bobby and Warren were three I was so happy to see too.

We went down to Southern California a few times. Among the people we visited were cousin Bob and Helen. Gene and Delores were our Arizona stop and Shirley in Texas. In Louisiana we visited Stace, Karen and family. Evelyn and Clive were in Kansas. Brother Warren and family were in Missouri. Shirley drove us from Texas once to visit Warren in Missouri. Warren played a trick on Glen by putting a pair of ladies panties in the guest bed were we were going to sleep. Shirley and Warren were laughing when we got up.

I told him, "You told me those sheets were clean!" I knew what he did. He always loved to play tricks.

My sisters Mary and Betty came over for the night. Betty got real sick.

We went to Teddy's in Iowa and visited with her and her daughter Kathie and family. We also got to see my brothers Charlie, Bobby and wife Margaret. We saw some of Glen's old Sea Bee buddies in Ohio and his cousin Doreen and Larry in Wyoming. In Montana we visited June, Steve and the kids. Utah was much more of a beautiful state than I ever remembered. Guess we just got there the right time of year. Donald was in Idaho and Gene and Delores and family and Ted in Oregon. In Washington we visited Randy and Claire, another Sea Bee buddy. Kenny and Lois were in Las Vegas. Glen liked visiting Lois because she always fixed him his favorite meal; fried chicken, potato salad and coleslaw. She always made him feel special. Kenny was like a son to him but he was his nephew. We always stopped at Glenda's in Lemore and stayed a few days. She has been in the Navy over fifteen years. Nora lives in Redding were the rest of the family lives. We loved going around visiting everyone.

One of our favorite places to visit was Apache Junction in Arizona. That is were Gene and Delores had their vacation home. We loved it so much we ended up buying a place there for ourselves. Our retirement home was dubbed Gold Vista. We didn't have the money to get it at first so Gene bought it for us until our money came in from the sales of our homes in Redding. Thanks Gene. We sure did have a lot of fun down there with you guys. We stayed there six winter months.

There was a Lutheran Church there we liked, almost as good as the one back in Redding. Glen wanted to make Gold Vista our permanent home he liked it so much. It was hard for me though. It was much too far away from all my kids. I was happy we had family there. Gene and Delores and Gene's cousins Gene and Delores Fry also lived there. We had lots of barbeques and functions going on all the time.

Then Glen was not feeling well and my back started bothering me quite a bit. All the packing to get there and packing to leave got to us both.

We traveled to Gold Beach Oregon quite a bit too. There were some little cabins over there right on the beach that we went back to several times. We would sit outside and look at the ocean. We would cook outside sometimes and the neighbors would join us. One time Gene and Delores came down when we there. There is nothing like Halibut on the barbeque out in the fresh air.

The little house we bought in Redding suited us just fine. It was small enough that we could just lock it up and go. We spent most of our time in Redding catching up with the family.

Our first year of marriage was a little tumultuous. All the family had to adjust to a new Mom or Dad and we had to adjust to each other. Glen was used to being boss and what he said was law. Well, wonder where I experienced that before. They say women many times marry men just like their father. Maybe that was the case for me too.

Unfortunately for him though, I was used to having things go my way for quite a few years so making this marriage work was going to take a lot of adjusting. We did not need any children problems. They were old enough to take care of themselves. You don't realize how many little things you do for your kids though until you have "yours and mine" at the same time. Things were different now. Mom or Dad weren't always available whenever they called or needed something they could always get before.

We needed our personal time and it was hard for a few of them, even as grown children. Now we were doing things that interested us and some of the kids actually felt a bit abandoned. As time went on though, everything adjusted; we to them, they to us and us to each other. This made our life much happier. It is much harder to adjust to change when you're older but we did it.

Shirley married Dennis, which added four more grandchildren to the list.

Glen and I were together all the time. He was my companion and he did not like me out of his site. I could not go any place without him. Traveling was fun for both of us. Boy did he love to travel. He would get up in the morning and plan our day on the road and off we would go on another adventure.

My little sister Teddy died of breast cancer. I'm so glad we went back to see her. June, Steve and family moved to Montana. We had a family reunion in Portland, Oregon. It was fun seeing most of the family. I had not seen my son Ted in a while or my granddaughter and grandson, Tonya and Scotty. Gene and Linda put on the reunion. Believe me they did a fantastic job. Everyone else helped out. Glena and I had it made. All we had to do was enjoy ourselves, and we sure did. What fun we had traveling up and down the coast, across the country, and anywhere Glen wanted to go. He loved being on the road. We went to Pat's birthday party in Sonoma. Pat is my granddaughter Linda's mother-in-law. Pat and I are good friends. She took Glen and I to several of the wineries around Sonoma and Napa. She would make Glen a big, and do I mean big martini and put all kinds of fruit in it. Boy did he love that. Glen bought her a dozen wine glasses from a winery that was closing out. He was so proud of the deal he got; twenty-five cents a glass.

It wasn't long after June and Steve moved to Montana that June was diagnosed with Parkinson's. This was devastating for all of us, and then to have her so far away. All any of us could think of was getting her back home and hoping somehow we could help.

In 2003 Glenda married Michael. Glen was so proud that he got to walk Glenda down the isle. Glen liked Michael quite a bit. They both like football and the Giants. Michael would call Glen and they would talk about the games. Michael had a heart attack five months later. What a tragedy. He died on Glenda's birthday. Glen missed Michael and their father-son chats. The games just weren't that much fun for him after that.

Mary had a brain tumor. She had an operation and recovered completely after about a year. I knew you could do it Mary.

Virginia's husband Fletcher died. He is now on a hill in Old Shasta on their place. Virginia and Fletcher were married sixty years.

Glen's health was beginning to fail faster and faster. Traveling back and forth was starting to wear him down. He was passing out a lot. The doctor could not find the right medicine for him and he was always trying something new. He had two stints and a pacemaker. He did fine for a while then he started passing out again. It was getting increasingly difficult for him to even get from one side of the room to the other. I got him a motorized wheel chair but he hardly ever used it.

June and Steve finally moved back to Redding. June's health is failing so rapidly and there is nothing I can do about it. I feel so helpless. I'm so glad she is here though. At least I can visit.

We sold the place in Apache Junction. We were happy and sad at the same time. It was too much going back and forth. I had an operation and came through with flying colors.

I still have a few aches and pains but nothing I can't live with. We went on short trips from then on. Sometimes just for a drive out to the lake. On the days he just couldn't leave the house he was really down.

In 2004 Glen fell again and this time he had to go to rehab for a month. Nora came every day and we played games. He looked forward to that. He had plenty of visitors. When he came home I got some assistance from Hospice. The caregivers were kind and considerate. They did a wonderful job of making our lives bearable. They touched my heart like angels from God. I could not have taken such good care of Glen without them. Each day was a treasure to us. Stace, our dear pastor, came every Thursday and had breakfast with Glen. This was a treasure for Glen and me. Glen planned what I should cook for breakfast even though he could not eat much of it. Plenty of friends and family came to visit but his Thursday breakfasts with Stace was what he looked forward to the most. There is not enough gold on this earth to buy those Thursdays for Glen. It was so generous of Stace to give that time to him every week. I will always appreciate that. I want to say thank you, to you Stace and your wife Karen. Your little boy Max was Glen's first grandchild. He was sure proud of him. I only wish he could have got to know Van and Katherine. Elaine Tree and Ed came twice a week and brought him a flower or some little thing they thought he would get a kick out of. The things he liked the most was this little stuffed dog Elaine brought him and a frog that Ed brought. Nora and the rest of the family came when they could, bringing him something they made or just for a visit. Glenda called often. Thank all of you for your time in making Glen's last days happy ones. He enjoyed your visits. He asked specifically to see Glenda and she came right away. She held his hand and sat patiently by his bedside. It was Thanksgiving morning. Most of the kids came over. Glen was very restless. I sat by his bed and held his hand. At nine o'clock Thanksgiving Day 2004 Glen died. I will miss him so. I am so glad he isn't suffering anymore.

That seven years with Glen came and went in an instant. He was good to me and we had a lot of fun in the short time we had together. I felt very empty when he died. That is when I really started writing about my life. It has been such good therapy for me.

In 2005 Elaine married Steven. They had been together ten years and I was glad to see them finally tie the knot.

Virginia gave up driving so I am taking her to the nutrition center once a week. This is something we both enjoy. We also go a lot of other places together. We always enjoy each other's company. Some days all I want to do is stay home and do nothing but write so I do. Boy do I like to write. Virginia and I are planning on painting again. I have been very busy with church, family, friends, writing, grandchildren and children visiting. There is very little time for me to get lonely. I am always on the go.

June is failing and it is so hard for me to see her lying helpless in her bed. She cannot talk, feed herself, wipe a tear away or even speak. But we do have conversations. I know her looks, and we can spell out things to each other. The other day she told me she loved me via the alphabet chart Steve made for her. That was so precious to me. I love to make her laugh. Arlene and I are there almost every day. We talk and share stories. Sometimes Steve will put in a video of old times. It's always a good visit; especially when we can make her laugh. I know she has mixed emotions about us coming over because she does not want anyone to see her that way and she definitely does not want anyone's pity. When we come to visit, we see past her illness though and come to visit just like we did before she even got sick. Steve takes care of all her needs and I am so grateful to him for that. I pray every day that God will help me to do something for her to make her happy or ease her pain in any way. It's really hard for me to accept sometimes that I am so healthy and she is not. June has always been so health conscience and has taken care of her family so well. I hate to see this happening to her. The only way I can get through it is to rely on God to give me the strength. I know he is helping her endure.

Sometimes at night in my living room I just sit and remember all the things I've had to endure but none of them compare to what my little June is going through.

I miss Glen. We had a lot of good times together in those seven short years. With Glen gone it is harder to cope with my problems alone. I so want to do something for June but all I can do is visit her and try to bring her a little cheer. I take the boys sometimes, I know it is hard for them. I talk with them sometimes and tell them there is no explanation of why some are afflicted and why some are not but it won't always be that way.

I have grandchildren marrying and having children of their own. Life has a funny way of repeating itself. I have so many wonderful people in my life who put up with me and all my imperfections. I have been blessed with a great family and good friends. No matter how old you get to be there will always be something happening in your life good or bad. All I can say is put your trust in God and live the best you can. Try to help those around you that are in need but don't forget to help yourself too. This was always hard for me. Someone else was always first. That is good to a certain degree but don't neglect yourself. But you know what? I think I might just be getting the hang of it now, I think. It's not over yet. Who knows what is in store for me.

In 2005 we had another family reunion. This time California was the host and Susan and Parrish had the reunion at their house. They did a great job. What a wonderful family I have, and they all belong to me. We plan to have a reunion every three years now. The next one is in 2008. I have been involved in so many people's lives, taking care of this one and that one. I think it is time for me to take care of me.

There are too many problems with so many people and I could never even begin to fix them all so I have to put it out of my mind. That's the problem though. I have never been one to relax for too long. I have come to the conclusion that I am actually helping my family by taking care of myself.

I am still living in that little house that Glen and I bought and it suits me just fine. It's remarkable how it resembles the very first house I lived in after moving away from home. It was even built by the W.P.A. in 1941 and it is written on the sidewalk out front. My Dad told me about the W.P.A. all those years ago when Roosevelt started the program to help people earn a living. When the Shasta Dam was being built they needed housing for the worker's so they built this little Dam House (that's what they called them) with W.P.A. workers. It sure brought back a lot of memories of my dad telling me about Social Security and the W.P.A.

My son-in-law Mike built the deck on the back of the house which turned out to be bigger than the house itself. Then he put a roof on the front porch. I don't know which I like better, thanks Mike.

There is always something that needs to be done at my little house and I am so glad that I always have "Kids to the Rescue". I love my little dollhouse. It's not only in the nicest neighborhood but I have the nicest mailman too. His name is Marc. Not only does Marc greet me with a smile each time he delivers my mail, he also takes care of all my mail when I am away. He always takes time out to say hi or comment on what a beautiful day it is or tell me how nice my yard looks. Actually, Marc feels more like one of my grandson's than my mailman. Thanks Marc, for just being you.

I am eighty-one years young and I consider myself so fortunate. I see some people the same age as me that seem so much older. I have all my teeth (except for one), I can still drive my car and most of the time I can remember where I parked it when I come out of the grocery store. Some of my daughters have admitted they already have a problem with that one. Best part of it is, I can take care of myself. Who could ask for anything more? My life is still like a bowl of cherries; beautiful and sweet with a few pits along the way. Thank God for my wonderful family and friends. I truly have been blessed.

I wrote my life story for my brothers and sisters, to show them what went on in my life after I left home. I also wrote it for my children; to let them know I love them. You can never say I love you enough. I never said it enough when they were little. It's never too late though. I love you kids, each and every one of you.

It took me about a year to write this. I have to finish it soon. Grandpa, Grandma, Mom, Dad, three sisters, a brother, a great grandson, three brother-in-laws, two sister-in-laws, a niece, two son-in-laws and four husbands all gone. Four husbands! I never in all my life thought that I would have been married four times; cherries and pits all in the same bowl!

Where did all the time go? My sister Mary, brother Warren and I are all in our eighties, Charlie is close behind and my little baby brother Bobby is already in his seventies.

Many of my children are older than I ever imagined I would be.

I have children ranging from the seventies to the forties.

For so many years I looked forward to the time when I would actually have a little time for myself. Now, with my children so involved in their own lives, their own children and grandchildren, I must admit I look forward to every precious moment I can spend with any of them.

I figured out a way to enjoy the home I'm living in and get paid for it too. Reverse Mortgaging my house is a decision I have not regretted yet. Ron and Patty Plum helped me out with that and I am plum happy. Now I can have the financial freedom that I worked for all my life. My children are very happy for me too. They are proud of me for how well I am taking care of myself. Sorry kids, there won't be much left for you, I'm taking as much as I can get now. They all tell me they would much rather see me enjoying what I have than trying to save something for them to fight over when I'm gone. Besides, anything I know that I have and they really want I say, "Take it, that much less clutter for me." I left my body to science because I know somebody might be able to use some spare parts. Warren's grandson P.J. needed a kidney at five years old. I don't want some kid to go without what they need if I can provide. It would be wonderful to help someone live as long as me. I thank God for my wonderful life.

The other day I was sitting on my front porch sipping a cup of tea, enjoying the wonderful cool breeze and reminiscing. I started thinking about how things began and how they turned out for each and every one of my children and realized there where some very interesting conclusions.

My oldest sons, Gene and Don are still more than just stepchildren, they are my friends. They still enjoy spending time with the family and playing music. In fact Gene has his own band and plays gigs for fun and profit. He and his band even have their own CD's!

Remember when Shirley was so interested in sewing as a child? She has been a very accomplished seamstress for years. In fact, she hopes to retire in a few years and give more attention to her creative side. She has some wonderful ideas for projects that could include costumes, uniforms, and even fashion items for pets.

My little yard lover Diana loves to dig in the dirt to this day. You should see her yard. I am so proud of her. Her yard is neat as a pin and beautifully organized. She has a real knack for knowing what goes with what and where to plant flowers or shrubs where they grow the best. She enjoys working in the yard and it shows.

My little Eddie used to love to tinker and still does. Ed is the Facilities Maintenance Manager for a Senior complex and he runs a tight ship. All the residents that live there love Ed because he is not only a kind and caring person, but he takes care of business and enjoys his work.

Arlene was an entertainer as a youngster and still is. Aside from her regular job she enjoys putting information to music and performing at reunions and retirements.

My little June who was so fussy about what she ate, turned out to be our first and only total vegetarian. June became very skilled in the preparation of delicious vegetarian dishes.

Ted grew up to be a very responsible and kind man. He sets a wonderful example for his children and is soon to be a grandpa for the first time. He eventually learned how to play a real guitar instead of a shovel and he enjoys singing and playing the guitar at our family reunions.

Lorrie was my little homemaker and grew up to be one. Lorrie enjoys working in the kitchen and has been gainfully employed planning menus and advising facilities on nutrition.

Elaine went to Cosmetology School and has enjoyed working as a hair stylist.

Diana's stepdaughter Virginia bought the restaurant we used to run in Cottonwood, Laura's Kitchen, and she named it Gramma's BBQ. She is doing well there.

Well, I could go on and on. Actually, I plan to go on and on as long as I can … but not with this story.

Who knows, maybe I'll come up with a sequel.

Mission Possible

My life is a mission and nothing is impossible,
After all I have God on my side.
I have been happy, sad, grief stricken and rich.
I have always been rich in life; a few pains
But general good health.
I've hurt a few people along the way and made a few happy.
I have the love of a great family and friends.
I learned to love, not hate.
Every one has some one they love.
What ever success I had in life came from God.
God gave me:
The strength to battle with difficulties and over come them.
Grace enough to confess my sins
Patience enough to toil until some good is accomplished
Charity enough to see good in all
Faith enough to remove all anxious fears concerning my future
Wealth enough to support my needs.

MY FAMILY

RELATIONSHIP	NAME	BORN	DIED	HOW	PRESIDENT	EXTRAS
Grandpa Mom's side	John Todd	1866	1938	Auto Accident	Ulysses S. Grant	I loved Grandpa very much
Grandma Mom's side	Laura Edwards Todd	1874	1951	Heart	Ulysses S. Grant	
Grandpa Dad's side	Albert Van Bibber	1848	1915	Stroke	Grover Cleveland	Never knew him Born in Holland
Grandma Dad's side	Phoebe Elizabeth Eakin Van Bibber	1853	1910	Heart	Millard Fillmore	Never knew her Born in Holland
Father Mom & Dad were married in Independence, Kansas May 21, 1912.	John Van Bibber	1892	1962	Heart	Grover Cleveland	Believed men should rule family and he sure did. I never crossed him. I loved & respected my dad
Mother They were married for 60 years Mom 15 Dad 19	Della Todd Van Bibber	1886	1971	Heart	Grover Cleveland	A cute, tiny little lady with a sweet nature and a big heart. I loved mom.
Uncle (Dad's Brother)	Oscar Van Bibber	1890	1959	Heart	Grover Cleveland	Lived with us off and on. His wife died giving birth to son Edgar.
Aunt	Meadie Showalder	1888	1956	Heart		Helped Uncle Oscar raise his son. She was good to all of us kids.

RELATIONS HIP	NAME	BORN	DIED	HOW	PRESIDENT	EXTRAS
Uncle	Arlie Showalder	1886	1952	Heart		They visited often. We were very close to them and enjoyed having him around.
Aunt (Mom's younger sister)	Mable Van Bibber Gnader	1899	2002	Heart		Lived the longest of all family 103. She and Frank had seven children. We grew up with them.
Cousin Aunt Meadie and Uncle Arlie's daughter.	Ethel Showalder Shivley	1899	1988	Heart		Had twin girls that are handicapped. Jean & Joan going strong at 71.
Sister	Lela Van Bibber Cunningham	1914	1988	Heart	Warren G. Harding	A good sister, We laughed a lot together
Sister	Mary Van Bibber Bray	1916			Warren G. Harding	A sister anyone would be proud of
Brother	Albert Van Bibber	1921	1949	Auto Accident	Warren G. Harding	Serviced overseas and got malaria
Me	Laura Van Bibber Roza Feise Shearer Dork	1925			Calvin Coolidge	Still going strong With more grandkids than I can count
Brother	John (Warren) Van Bibber	1926			Calvin Coolidge	Was an M.P. in the Marines. My best buddy in life.
Brother	Charlie Van Bibber	1928	2008	Cancer	Calvin Coolidge	Charlie was a loner. I understand now, Warren and I were always gone. I love you Charlie.
Sister	Thelma (Teddy) Jane Van Bibber Rolfe	1930	2000	Cancer	Calvin Coolidge	I remember Teddy mostly in my teen years. We got reacquainted when we got older.

RELATIONS HIP	NAME	BORN	DIED	HOW	PRESIDENT	EXTRAS
Sister	Bonnie Lou Van Bibber	1932	1932	Infant Death		Poor Bonnie Lou. We were all heartbroken.
Brother	Robert (Bobby) Lindy Van Bibber	1935			Franklin Roosevelt	Quite easy going like mom. Little Bobby truly never knew me but I knew him. What a sweetheart he was. I loved him very much. My darling little baby brother.
Sister	Bessie (Betty) Van Bibber Cusic	1923	1993	Cancer	Calvin Coolidge	For some unknown reason we were never close but I always loved her. She had bad health
Sister	Edna Mae Van Bibber	1913	1913	Infant Death		I didn't really even know her.
1st Husband Lived a hard life and died young.	Edward Rosa	1924	1961	Cirrhosis of the Liver	Calvin Coolidge	Too bad he missed out on his three beautiful children by ruining his life with alcohol abuse
2nd Husband We were married 31 years I always called him my first husband. We had a full life together.	Arthur Theodore Feise	1907	1981	Cancer	Theodore Roosevelt	He loved being a carpenter and a cowboy. We had five children. He smoked a lot. He died of cancer. So think before you take the first puff.

RELATIONS HIP	NAME	BORN	DIED	HOW	PRESIDENT	EXTRAS
3rd Husband Such a short marriage, three weeks.	William Shearer	1924	1995	Cancer	Calvin Coolidge	I only knew him for one year and three months before we were married. He was a very nice man.
4th Husband Last but not least man in my life.	Glen Dork	1919	2004	Heart	Woodrow Wilson	What a lot of fun we had in seven short years. Yes, we were "The Traveling Dorks"
Son	Eugene Feise	11/6/28			Calvin Coolidge	Arch's first son. We have always been very good friends.
Daughter-In-Law	Delores Marty Feise	5/16/32			Calvin Coolidge	No one could ask for a nicer daughter-in-law.
Son	Donald Feise	6/5/30			Calvin Coolidge	Arch's second son. We have always been very good friends.
Daughter-In-Law and Niece	Elnora Cunningham Feise	7/10/41			Franklin Roosevelt	I loved her like one of my own daughters. Still do.
Niece	Evelyn Cunningham Meairs	3/7/39			Franklin Roosevelt	What a sweet, kind, friend. Like a daughter to me too.
Nephew-In-Law	Clive Meairs	10/13/37			Franklin Roosevelt	Has always helped out whenever he could. Love you.
Nephew	Howard Cunningham	4/20/36			Franklin Roosevelt	We have always been good friends.
Niece-In-Law	Donna Cunningham		1966	Heart failure		Was one of my favorite girlfriends.

RELATIONS HIP	NAME	BORN	DIED	HOW	PRESIDENT	EXTRAS
Daughter	Nora Dork Lee Dork	12/23/50			Harry Truman	Glen's oldest daughter No children but has a dog named Keno
Daughter	Glenda Dork Nasipak Parkhurst	8/10/59			Harry Truman	Glen's youngest daughter In the Navy for 15 years. Has a dog named Bud.
Daughter	Shirley Louise Roza Feise Donarski McKensie	11/28/46			Franklin Roosevelt	My first daughter Always something special about your first child.
Son-In-Law	Dennis McKenzie	9/36/36			Franklin Roosevelt	A fine son-in-law
Daughter	Diana Jean Feise Harris	12/21/47			Harry Truman	Daughter #2 My sweet tiny little baby
Son-In-Law	Bill Harris		2000	Cancer		A fine son-in-law
Son	Edward Bernard	8/22/49			Harry Truman	My first little baby Boy. He thought he came in a Kellogg's box.
Daughter-In-Law	Doris Feise					A fine daughter-in-law
Daughter	Arlene Elizabeth Feise Myers Hursey Robinson	10/27/51			Harry Truman	My 3rd daughter A daddy's girl.
Son-In-Law	Mel Robinson	12/29/50			Harry Truman	A fine son-in-law
Daughter	June Marie Feise Yorks	6/16/53	7/17/07	Parkinsons	Harry Truman	Daughter #4. A mama's girl
Son-In-Law	Steve Yorks	9/28/50			Harry Truman	A fine son-in-law
Son	Alan Theodore (Ted) Feise	10/25/54			Harry Truman	My 2nd little tiny baby boy.

RELATIONSHIP	NAME	BORN	DIED	HOW	PRESIDENT	EXTRAS
Daughter	Lorraine Mae (Lorrie) Feise Vollmer Oglesby McDonald	6/21/57			Harry Truman	Thought for sure she was going to be my last baby. My fifth little girl.
Son-In-Law	Mike McDonald	2/21/51			Harry Truman	A fine son-in-law
Daughter	Elaine Lea Feise Toothman Hoffman	10/13/62			John F. Kennedy	Surprise! My 6th little baby girl
Son-In-Law	Steven Hoffman	2/24/48			Harry Truman	A fine son-in-law
Niece	Beth Cunningham Meurer	7/27/57			Harry Truman	Donna & Howard Cunningham's
Nephew-In-Law	Jim Meurer	7/18/57			Harry Truman	
Nephew	Jonathan Meurer	2/24/82				
Niece	Brooke Meurer	2/1/81				
Nephew	Matthew Meurer	2/21/84				
Niece	Kim Cunningham Hake	7/28/59				Donna & Howard Cunningham's
Nephew-In-Law	Don Hake					
Niece	Heidi Hake					
Nephew	Ryan Hake					
Niece	Carley Hake					
Nephew	Jeff Cunningham	1961				Donna & Howard Cunningham's
Niece-In-Law	Jo Cunningham	11/7/63				
Niece	Jessica Cunningham	10/13/86				
Niece	Jennifer Cunningham	7/1/88				

RELATIONS HIP	NAME	BORN	DIED	HOW		EXTRAS
Pastor	Stace Rollefson	9/23/65				Like a son to Glen and now to me
Pastor's Wife	Karen Rollefson	7/31/68				
Niece	Lela Meairs Hill	3/14/65				Evelyn & Clive Meairs
Nephew	Wayne Meairs III	12/30/62				Evelyn & Clive
Niece	Dora Meairs	11/13/69				Evelyn & Clive
Granddaughter	Joanne Feise Sharon	6/5/54				Gene & Delores Feise
Grandson In-Law	Dave Sharon	3/21/45				
Granddaughter	Linda Feise Martz	7/14/55				Gene & Delores
Grandson In-Law	Jon Martz	6/28/55				
Grandson	James Feise	11/20/58				Gene & Delores
Granddaughter In-Law	Dona Feise	11/1				
Grandson	Brett Feise	3/18/63				Don & Elnora Feise
Granddaughter	Louise Feise Pico	5/15/65				Don & Elnora
Grandson In-Law	Joe Pico	2/14/61				
Granddaughter	Susan Feise Berlic Malson	3/27/69				Don & Elnora
Grandson In-Law	Parrish Malson	8/10/61				
Granddaughter	Christine Donarski Lindsey Brinneman	8/6/68				Shirley & Art Donarski
Grandson In-Law	Larry Brinneman	8/15/65				
Granddaughter	Sharon Donarski Nilsson	8/27/69				Shirley & Art
Grandson In-Law	Kurt Nilsson	6/1/67				
Grandson	Michael Donarski	8/15/72				Shirley & Art

RELATIONSHIP	NAME	BORN	DIED	HOW		EXTRAS
Granddaughter In-Law	Katie Donarski	12/19/74				
Granddaughter	Denise Donarski Armstrong	8/19/72				Shirley & Art
Grandson In-Law	Greg Armstrong	1970				
Granddaughter	Virginia Harris					Bill Harris
Granddaughter	Amy Harris Kennedy	7/11/72				Diana & Bill Harris
Grandson In-Law	Trevor Kennedy	9/3/70				
Grandson	Bill Pyatt	7/7/80				Doris Pyatt Feise
Grandson	Josh	9/21/91				Doris Pyatt Feise
Grandson	Cory Feise	6/22/72				Ed & Annette Feise
Granddaughter	Cheri Myers Scordel	4/6/72				Bob & Arlene Myers/Feise
Grandson In-Law	Tom Scordel	2/25/68				
Granddaughter	Tiffany Robinson	12/14/81				Mel Robinson
Granddaughter	Alaina Robinson	7/1/84				Mel Robinson

RELATIONSHIP	NAME	BORN	DIED	HOW	WHO'S KID	EXTRAS
Granddaughter	Cyera Yorks	1/1/88			June & Steve Yorks	
Grandson	Skylar Yorks	10/11/90			June & Steve	
Grandson	Michael Yorks	11/30/93			June & Steve	
Grandson	Scott Feise	10/7/72			Ted & Cindy Feise	
Granddaughter	Tonya Feise	5/9/78			Ted & Cindy	
Great Grandson	Nicholas	2007			Tonya & Viktor	
Grandson In-Law	Viktor					
Granddaughter	Shannon Vollmer Brown Crain	4/25/76			Lorrie & Darren Vollmer	

RELATIONS HIP	NAME	BORN	DIED	HOW	WHO'S KID	EXTRAS
Grandson In-Law	Dave Crain	2/26/76				
Granddaughter	Natasha Vollmer Oglesby Dial	7/16/75			Lorrie & Darren	
Grandson In-Law	Larry Dial	9/29/69				
Granddaughter	Leah Oglesby	1/16/80			Lorrie & Tom Oglesby	
Grandson	Sean Oglesby	1/16/82			Lorrie & Tom	
Grandson	T.J. McDonald	12/26/76			Mike McDonald	
Granddaughter	Holly McDonald Johnson	5/1/74			Mike McDonald	
Grandson In-Law	Eric Johnson	10/19/74				
Grandson	Andrew Toothman	1/30/86			Elaine & Larry Toothman	
Granddaughter	Nicole Toothman	11/7/88			Elaine & Larry	
	Max Rollefson	6/30/94			Stace & Karen	
	Kathyran Rollefson	11/13/01			Stace & Karen	
	Van Rollefson	10/27/99			Stace & Karen	
	Alex Malson	8/10/61			Parrish Malson	
	Andy Malson	8/15/89				
	Arron Malson	8/13/91				
Great Granddaughter	Kristen Martz	6/18/85			Gene & Delores	Linda & Jon Martz
Great Granddaughter	Allison Martz	9/29/86			Gene & Delores	Linda & Jon
Great Great Grandson	Micah	2006			Gene & Delores	Allison &
Great Granddaughter	Emile Martz	11/6/94			Gene & Delores	Linda & Jon
Great Granddaughter	Mallory Martz	2/18/97			Gene & Delores	Linda & Jon
Great Grandson	Richard Sharon				Gene & Delores	Joanne & Dave Sharon

RELATIONSHIP	NAME	BORN	DIED	HOW	WHO'S KID	EXTRAS
Great Granddaughter	Aliece Sharon				Gene & Delores	Joanne & Dave
Great Granddaughter	Samantha Feise	3/2/99			Gene & Delores	Jim & Dona Feise
Great Granddaughter	Katheryn Feise	9/23/03			Gene & Delores	Jim & Dona
Great Grandson	Bryce Pico	12/14/88			Don	Louise & Joe Pico
Great Granddaughter	Ellie Pico	5/16/95			Don	Louise & Joe
Great Granddaughter	Carrie Pico	5/15/87			Don	Louise & Joe
Great Granddaughter	Brooke Pico	5/10/86			Don	Louise & Joe
RELATIONSHIP	NAME	BORN	DIED	HOW	Who's kid	EXTRAS
Great Grandson	Todd Scrima	1988	1991	Drowned	Don	Susan & Todd Scrima
Great Grandson	Nicolas Scrima	3/11/90			Don	Susan & Todd
Great Granddaughter	Kennedy Berlic	7/28/98			Don	Susan & Jerry Berlic
Great Grandson	William Berlic	11/19/99			Don	Susan & Jerry
Great Grandson	Brandon Berlic	12/15/95			Don	Susan & Jerry
Great Granddaughter	Courtney Buckley	11/13/69			Shirley	Christine & Larry
Great Granddaughter	Cloe	2007			Courtney	Courtney & Trenton
Great Grandson	Branden Lindsey	2/20/92			Shirley	Christine & Larry
Great Grandson	Shawn Brinneman	2/7/91			Shirley	Christine & Larry
Great Granddaughter	Ashley Brinneman	2/20/92			Shirley	Christine & Larry

RELATIONS HIP	NAME	BORN	DIED	HOW	WHO'S KID	EXTRAS
Great Grandson	Jonah Nilsson	4/8/95			Shirley	Kurt & Sharon Nilsson
Great Grandson	Griffen Nilsson	5/16/97			Shirley	Kurt & Sharon
Great Grandson	Sawyer Nilsson	3/11/01			Shirley	Kurt & Sharon
Great Grandson	Michael Donarski Jr.	3/6/96			Shirley	Mike & Katie Donarski
Great Granddaughter	Jobie Donarski	1/9/00			Shirley	Mike & Katie
Great Granddaughter	Hanna Armstrong	10/7/99			Shirley	Denise & Greg Armstong
Great Granddaughter	Chelsea	11/11/93			Shirley	Denise & Greg
Great Granddaughter	Jenny Kiras	11/5/84			Shirley	
Great Granddaughter	Julie Zdonek	7/17/89			Shirley	
Great Granddaughter	Caitlin Rocchi	5/18/89			Shirley	
Great Granddaughter	Isabella Kennedy	3/13/02			Diana	Amy & Trevor Kennedy
Great Grandson	Tommy Scordel	2/3/01			Arlene	Cheri & Tom Scordel
Great Granddaughter	Elizabeth Scordel	8/2/03			Arlene	Cheri & Tom
Great Granddaughter	Kaylea Brown	10/28/90			Lorrie	Shannon & Scott Brown
Great Granddaughter	Allie Crain	10/9/98			Lorrie	Shannon & Dave Crain
Great Granddaughter	Brooklyn Leah June	1/07			Lorrie	Shannon & Dave
Great Granddaughter	Ashley Dial	12/27/91			Lorrie	Natasha & Larry Dial
Great Granddaughter	Taylor Dial	2/15/93			Lorrie	Natasha & Larry

RELATIONSHIP	NAME	BORN	DIED	HOW	WHO'S KID	EXTRAS
Great Granddaughter	Meriah Johnson	2/15/93			Lorrie	Holly & Eric Johnson
Great Grandson	Blaine Johnson	4/7/80			Lorrie	Holly & Eric
Great Grandson	Jordan Johnson	10/3/84			Lorrie	Holly & Eric
Great Granddaughter	Georgia	2004			Don	Joe & Louise Pico

Close Friends		Born	Died
	Virginia Mc Comb	8/30/19	
	Darlene Wolcott	1928	
	Elwyn Wolcott	1925	
	Geneva Hanson	1935	
	Kitty Bare	1939	
	Jim Humiston	1925	2007
	Lorraine Humiston	1925	
	Sharon Parker		
	Bill & Doris Buckhorn		
	Paul & Norma		
	Margaret Gardener		
	Bob Gardener	1920	2007
	Don & Ethellen Shell		
	Heather (Virgina's daughter)		
	Caroline	1923	2006
	Claudene	1925	
	Pat Eckmam		
	Don & Lois Kraft		
	Gene & Delores Fry		
	Kitty Bare		
	Geneva Johnson		

978-0-595-50003-1
0-595-50003-X